Help yourself to learning at work

Julia Waldman

RHP

Russell House Publishing

First published in 1999 by

Russell House Publishing Limited
4 St. George's House
Uplyme Road Business Park
Lyme Regis
Dorset
DT7 3LS

British Library Cataloguing-in-Publication Data:
A catalogue record for this book is available from the
British Library

ISBN 1-898924-44-9

Typeset by TW Typesetting, Plymouth, Devon

Printed by Cromwell Press, Trowbridge

Russell House Publishing

is a group of social work, probation, education and
youth and community work practitioners working
in collaboration with a professional publishing
team. Our aim is to work closely with the field to
produce valuable and innovative materials to help
managers, trainers, practitioners and students. We
are keen to receive feedback on publications and
new ideas for future projects.

Contents

For my parents,
René and Grace
with love and thanks.

Acknowledgements

Thanks to:

Keith, Jamie, Holly, Robin and Ryan for putting up
with me disappearing to work.

Veronica Tippetts for wading through a full first draft.

All the practitioners and students I have tried things
out on and worked with, and especially my 1997–99
tutor group, Lisa Coombes, Jonty Fairhead, Nicky
Glover, Liz King, Andy Markland, Sarah Newman,
Caroline Triggs and Mark Venning.

Shirley Fletcher for showing me that less can
sometimes mean more.

Ann Wheal for helping me get the ball rolling.

Russell House Publishing for their patience and
encouragement.

Many children, women and young people who have
made me rethink and made the learning worthwhile.

About the author

Julia Waldman currently works with a human resource consultancy, for the Social Work Department at the University of Southampton, the Open University and as an independent researcher and consultant. Her work focuses on using research and human resource development to improve work-based policies and practice in a variety of occupational areas. She has had a portfolio career that has included community and youth work, playwork social care, adult education, higher education, community activism, travelling and being a mature student with a family.

Introduction

Who is this book for?

In thinking about the audience for this book I knew almost immediately that I wanted it to be for people who are learning within their places of work – whether that work is paid or unpaid. It is for those who are *doing* the learning.

I identified three groups with different needs who I anticipated might use the book. They are:

- Students undertaking internal or external education or training programmes in which they may need more help to link learning with practice, perhaps on a practice placement or as part of a secondment.
- Managers, practitioners or volunteers, or people who combine paid and upaid roles, who have a concern for their own professional development and who want to find ways of maintaining a critical and developmental edge to their work activities. They may need either fresh ideas or reminding of techniques, contexts and knowledge to help them sharpen perspectives on practice.
- People starting out in community, social care work or related occupations who see paid or unpaid work experience as a career bridge. They may need to convince admissions tutors or panels on professional qualifying programmes that they have the necessary awareness of issues and thinking skills to learn from formal courses. Or they may be involved in vocational work-based qualifications.

This book will help each of these groups who are grappling with the day-to-day demands of learning and working simultaneously.

Using work experience in a critical way may also help people to decide whether their career choice is really the best one for them.

Why write this book?

Contemporary ideas about lifelong learning encourage us to feel that we should all be learning throughout our lives. Within this vision the workplace is just one of many learning environments available to us for continuing personal and professional development. Homes, communities, institutions . . . every situation is a potential place in which to learn.

The workplace is, of course, a learning context ripe for lifelong professional learning. Such learning might be formal, in that it constitutes a recognised

1

programme of training or development; or it might be described as informal, perhaps driven by a desire for personal or professional growth. The second is no less important than the first. In either circumstance, and the shades in between, the day-to-day activities of the workplace contribute directly to what and how we can learn at work.

From my own experience I believe that an approach to learning that involves practicing (working) and practising (developing skills, knowledge and understanding) at the same time, places special demands on individuals to make the most of the opportunities that may present themselves.

Through working with students, employees and others in a wide variety of work settings, I have researched, developed and used a range of learning aids that are incorporated in this book.

The context of learning at work

It is naive to view the workplace as a breeding ground for enlightened personal growth, even for those who are very motivated! Many barriers may be put up, externally as well as internally, to block personal development. Simply having experience at work does not necessarily lead to people learning from that experience.

In the current tide of work-based human resource developments, a dominant perspective seems to be on assessment mechanisms linked to *performing* at work, for example through National Vocational Qualifications (S/NVQs), but not always on *learning*. Although such mechanisms allow individuals to demonstrate their learning based on what happens in their place of work, it is too often true that the individual is the passive recipient of the needs and requirements of others. These 'others' may include management, training and education providers and regulatory bodies.

Learning goals are constrained within frequently functional assessment tools that are driven by corporate needs, rather than set within a liberal framework of individual autonomy.

To deny the significance of this context in writing about a self-help approach to learning at work would diminish the relevance of the book. The material in the book will give the reader more ideas and confidence for learning within a culture of regulated standards and requirements that shows little sign of abating.

Developing a 'learner-outlook'

Having worked with students and practitioners in a range of settings and circumstances, I am aware of the vast differences amongst them in being able to harness fully their learning opportunities and how they can sometimes become sidetracked by other demands. These demands can compete to hold back our potential, as individuals, to learn from the things that are happening around us.

Of course the argument that there is too much to do and not enough time will often be put forward; that it is not possible to find space to reflect on events and/or record them in a systematic and meaningful way to help learning.

The stance that this book takes is that each of us needs to develop and maintain a personal interpretation of what I will refer to as a 'learner-outlook'; a perspective to be sustained at whatever stage of professional career development we may be at.

I have chosen to focus on the workplace as a learning environment in which we may, at any stage in a career, make choices related to personal and/or professional development. A learner-outlook may help in being prepared for, and making decisions about, those choices.

To adopt a common expression; a 'learner-outlook' is not just for initial professional education, it's for life!

Learning and working at the same time

Arguably, many current approaches to work-based learning give only limited attention to the reflective and critical components of learning. One of the limits of the emphasis on competences is that the learner has their eyes on the end of the road; the tick in the box endorsing them as 'competent'.

Many people will either miss or not be shown the opportunities that lie along the competency pathway, things which will probably enrich the journey's end. Even functional approaches give scope for being creative and for attending to learning processes as well as products. I hope this book will enable people to identify and utilise such opportunities.

Another aspect about work-based learning that is often played down is the challenge that it presents to the individual. In many ways it is much easier to go somewhere else to do your learning, away from the distractions of work. Many qualified professionals understand the value of going out of the workplace to secure time for space and reflection, to clear the mind of other matters and focus upon what may seem like the selfish task of personal learning. This dynamic may be especially relevant to staff working in the human services where the emotional demands may work against leaving a chink of mental creativity for personal development.

Most people have experience of work-based learning in some form. When children play at copying the parental figures in their lives they are practising the basics of learning by watching and doing. As adults, especially in formal work settings, these skills and attitudes towards learning may be implicit in what we do. But it is perhaps important to appreciate in explicit ways *how* we learn in order to extend the depth and usefulness of *what* we learn.

Using this book

The material in this book addresses a number of topics that are intended to provide both conceptual and practical tools to extend people's abilities to learn at work.

Chapter 1 defines the contemporary context and meaning of work-based learning in professional education and training, particularly for people working in community, health and social care settings. It presents a rationale and definition of a learner-outlook as a central focus of the book.

Chapter 2 identifies some theories and perspectives that are concerned with how adults learn and issues associated with learning at work. These are intended to provide insights into the processes of learning with which people can develop and refine their own learning style.

The following chapters take a more practical approach to learning at work by exploring the different facets of the work environment and the ways in which we can help ourselves to learn. The premise underlying these chapters is that each of us can take greater responsibility for our own learning and make better use of the resources available to us, both personal and external, to enhance our potential to learn.

Chapter 3 focuses on self-awareness and self-assessment activities for use and adaptation by individual learners in different work contexts. It addresses the personal dimensions of learning and how people can be their own curriculum guide.

Chapter 4 looks at the many forms of learning support available to us from all the people who cross our paths at work. It seeks to unravel and make explicit the different types of helping relationships that can be utilised at work. These may arise informally or be set within formal or contracted arrangements.

Chapter 5 provides a look at other resources that may be accessible to facilitate learning in the workplace. This may provide a reminder that the mundane and routine can be worthy of attention for use in a fresh way, whether creatively or critically. It also explores the opportunities created by, for example, the growth of information and communications technology.

Chapter 6 provides a way of bringing a research dimension to day-to-day work activities, as a means of extending the learner-outlook. It introduces 'action research' as a technically and ideologically accessible way to combine research and work activities. The last third of the chapter presents an example of designing a small-scale research project in the workplace.

Chapter 7 concludes the book by drawing away from personal experiences and looking towards the vision of lifelong learning and portfolio careers that the well-known management writer Charles Handy proposed would be the norm in the not too distant future.

Summary

I hope that the book will provide several ways of helping people to learn in a richer way at work by:

- Being a source of comfort, and an acknowledgement that learning at work is often hard to sustain.
- Providing practical activities readers can dip in and out of at different times.
- Suggesting new ways of tackling common and recurring dilemmas.
- Raising awareness of different learning pathways.
- Encouraging people to seek guidance and support regarding these different pathways.

This book is a personal response to my own attempts to grapple with the ongoing challenge of maintaining a 'learner-outlook'.

It is because I experienced, and continue to experience, the complexities and debates in a personalised way, as well as professionally, that I offer this book. I hope it opens windows that have been closed for some readers.

1. Learning and work: key themes and definitions

> *The highest reward of a person's toil is not what they get for it, but what they become by it.* John Ruskin cited in Warner (1999:170)

Any journey has a beginning, and for the one this book may take you on, it starts with an overview of its key themes. This chapter will introduce you to the approach to learning at work which is at the heart of the ideas and concepts presented in later chapters.

Key themes of the book

In summary these themes are:

- Learning at work is not a passive activity, but must involve critical engagement with day-to-day roles and tasks.
- Individuals learn all the time, but controlling how and what we learn at work requires sustained attention.
- An individual approach to learning is part of a learner-outlook, relevant at any stage of a career.
- Developing a learner-outlook as an integral part of good practice needs detailed explanation.
- Learning takes place within the context of the shifting sands of policy and practice in the human services.
- Learning environments affect how and what we as individuals learn.
- Ideas about learning are subject to political ideologies that make us vulnerable to external demands and pressure in work-based learning environments.

Defining learning at work

Work-based learning is an expression that, along with lifelong learning, continues to be reconstituted and applied to different education and training systems and policies.

Learning at work is nothing new. An apprentice model of technical and professional development is one that has spanned cultural and historical evolution. This book is concerned, however, with models and tools that are relevant to the contemporary practitioner, student and volunteer.

The two parts of the term 'work' and 'learning' are explored separately below.

What is work?

Work can be defined in many ways. It includes many activities, not all of which involve payment. Even if you do not have paid employment it is hoped you will identify with the definition used here and therefore feel that this book is of relevance to your situation.

The problems of defining work are, arguably, exacerbated when explored in the context of community, social and health care work. A distinction of employed or waged is insufficient to encompass the range of work roles and activities within the broad arena of the human services.

The role of a local authority foster carer, for instance shows the dilemmas of naming and labelling work, since the carer can be both a service user and a provider of services. A carer receives some money for the service, but is neither salaried nor strictly a volunteer.

The traditional urban distinction between 'home' and 'work' is also meaningless in the example above, and increasingly redundant as new technology and contemporary work patterns fragment the familiar linear and hierarchical nature of jobs and career pathways. This significant context to learning will be developed further in Chapters 2 and 7.

Individuals also define work differently, according to their motivations and needs. Work for some is simply a means to an end; the time it entails merely a lull in between 'real life' going on.

A contrasting perspective is of work as a vocation; as the driver; as the route to self-esteem, status and a sense of identity. These are, of course, simplistic polarisations. Attitudes towards work are also bound up by cultural, familial and social norms and expectations. There will be many factors holding people back from undertaking, as they perceive it, meaningful work, for example social exclusion or being differently abled. Supporting people over such barriers is one of the tasks many of us working in community and social work settings undertake.

Do you work to live or live to work?

Waged work is tied up with public identity, assigned by society and ascribed by the role(s) people undertake. It is also linked to institutionalised measures of success; salary levels, seniority, job status and power.

> *For many people who are not in waged work the impact may not be simply financial but it may also be deeply personal and informed by social definitions of who is an 'active' member of society. The unwaged carer who stays out of the employment market to care for a relative has historically been an invisible contributor to society. Carers may be actively working but the social construction of the role has been personalised, gendered and domesticised.*
> (Ranade, 1993, cited in Horwood, 1994)

Social policy is slowly grappling with a changing outlook that acknowledges the wider structural and social implications of such a role, that moves it away from the private sphere and towards greater recognition of its public contribution. Such recognition, however, should not be viewed in an uncritical way. For many carers the benefits of being more visible are blunted by a view that this is merely a cost-saving exercise in public services that does little to further the cause of social equality. Davis (1996:220), for example, cites the doubts expressed by groups like the National Carer's Association and Equal Opportunities Commission who point out that:

'family care' may be a euphemism for care by the nearest female relative.

Work, therefore, has not only an individual interpretation, but also a social definition that will vary across cultures, periods of history, race, gender and class.

Features of work

From acknowledging the problems of defining work, for the purposes of setting a framework for the material in this book some appropriate guidelines must be selected.

From the examples above it would appear that features of work include:

- Having a named role that is usually socially given.
- A relationship to others that is outside personal ties and including some kind of contractual (formal or informal) arrangement about the boundaries of that relationship.
- Tasks and activities that are concerned with more than the worker's personal survival needs and this usually means having a practice dimension.

Where does work happen?

So with this three-part definition, of which individuals may relate to one or more of these parts, the environment in which work takes place is open. It allows for:

- work at the worker's home
- work in the home of others
- work that is not linked to a building or place
- work that takes place in offices, other buildings or vehicles

Who works?

People who work may be one or more of the following:

- self-employed
- unwaged
- volunteering

- part-time employed
- full-time employed
- on fixed term contracts
- a student or trainee
- in a role representing others (e.g. councillor)

What does work involve?

It implies that a worker is someone who has some or all of the following:

- customers
- an employer
- a contractual (casual, formal, written, verbal) agreement with someone else to provide a task or service for another person or group for financial or other recognition
- an individual or body to whom there is some accountability for actions

Work is about additional tasks or activities that are more than for personal gain or reward. The definition above may exclude some activities and roles others may describe as work. It is a definition that is fit for the purpose; affirming that people who engage in duties, tasks and jobs with a social dimension can keep learning and improving in their work, an improvement that hopefully will benefit their service users or customers.

Rather than associating work with traditional indicators of success, such as salary or status, many people need to find alternative ways of measuring rewards and satisfaction. Often career plans are tied up with life plans. As mentioned at the start of the chapter, it is not sufficient in today's world to lay down a plan for a career and expect to follow it. As Dwyer (1995:14) reminds us 'It is wise to have a plan, but dangerous to see it as the plan'.

Part of a satisfactory route through a working life means being able to cope with the difficulties and upheavals that will need to be faced. The level of change many people now experience may mean that individually and collectively there is a need to find new ways of validating success in life.

Judging your success by the standards established by someone else may lead to a life of frustration. (Reece and Brandt, 1996:468)

A reality is, of course, that working life is becoming increasingly codified, monitored and driven by standards. It can be difficult to separate personal needs and aspirations from the goals which are required to be achieved on behalf of others.

Taking control of your learning as one of the key themes of this book is one way of trying to shift the balance of authority and direction on to a more favourable position. As is the concept of 'right livelihood' as a framework for thinking and acting with more autonomy. Reece and Brandt (1996) set out a description of right livelihood, based on the work of Marsha Sinetar and Michael Phillips. They identify three characteristics to 'right livelihood':

Conscious choice. For many people conscious choice is difficult because it means learning to act not on what others say and want, but on the choices you want to make based on the things you value. This can take courage to face your fears about those choices and their implications.

Money comes second. A narrow definition of success that is based only on money may be counter-productive because other definitions of rewards are sidelined and success is externalised rather than coming from within.

Work is a vehicle for self-expression. This is concerned with the need in people for a sense of purpose in what they do, that in whatever sphere of work they are, work can be used as a medium for growth and greater self-awareness.

These ideas may seem to be removed from the realities of people's working lives. Reece and Brandt (1996) argue, however, that people who choose right livelihood have a number of features in common. They:

- are self-disciplined
- set realistic and meaningful goals
- recognise when they are achieving their goals and the satisfaction they are gaining in the process
- have defined their relationship with money
- have enough self-esteem to act on their choices

Ideas about right livelihood do not mean ignoring the considerable barriers that many people have to overcome in their private and working lives. They illustrate, however, that working towards personal choice means reflecting, planning, learning, acting and growing. Later on in this book there are ideas designed to help you to take these steps and they may help you in your own journey towards your own right livelihood.

Some definitions of learning

Now that a context about work has been provided, the same must be done for 'learning'. It is important to be explicit about what learning means because in a competency culture it is possible to mistake demonstrating a standard in a particular work activity as learning. This refers to an output that is a product of a number of elements, of which learning will only be one.

Alan Rogers (1992:9) summarises learning as follows:

Learning means making changes – in our knowing, thinking, feeling and doing. Some of these changes are permanent, others are for a time only. Learning arises from our experiences. It takes different forms.

So learning is a personal process. The sum of each person's learning will be different. Assessments usually only look at the evidence for one or several parts of the total learning sum so it helps if you can be your own assessor too.

Learning as a continuum of meaning

Carl Rogers (1983:20) describes two general types of learning along what he refers to as a *continuum of meaning*. At one extreme is the learning that has no personal connection with the learner whatsoever and at the other is experiential learning rooted in meaning and significance. He conveys his support of experiential learning as follows:

> *Significant learning combines the logical* **and** *the intuitive, the intellectual* **and** *the feelings, the concept* **and** *the experience, the idea* and *the meaning. When we learn in that way we are* **whole.**

Learning, therefore, is a change in yourself that effects a change in some or all of your work activities. The *need* to learn, though not what you *actually* learn, may be imposed upon you as an individual. It can also be self-generated and welcomed or conversely resisted. These contexts are critical to learning.

The stance of this book is that essentially learning is something to be welcomed but that individuals need to feel empowered within any learning process. This can be facilitated by access to appropriate information, guidance, support, resources and, crucially, ensuring the learner owns the learning requirements and opportunities that present.

Rogers' continuum of meaning in learning is a helpful tool for critiquing the nature of the learning you experience. The emphasis within this book is upon the connective and holistic in Rogers' experiential zone. Even learning a practical skill should inevitably generate some kind of chain reaction to other thoughts and feelings as part of wider self-development.

Help with making connections for learning

Such connectivity, may need to be helped along. The material is intended to be pragmatic in its focus, so that learning is rooted in lived realities rather than as an objectified theorising of issues.

Combining work and learning

Having defined work and learning separately, this section concludes by indicating that learning at work means using the situations and events that arise from the activities you undertake at your place of work as the medium to facilitate learning.

Developing a learner-outlook

The idea of the autonomous and experientially-challenged learner is encompassed within the key theme of the learner-outlook. Throughout the book there will be ideas and activities for widening this learner-outlook. This in essence represents a way of looking at the world. It is about individuals valuing their own thoughts and feelings and combining these with the necessary objectivity to both be part of a learning situation whilst anticipating the next. A learner-outlook means maintaining a conscious reflexivity to lifelong learning as part of a professional or working persona. As the saying goes, 'you can live 100 years or live the same year 100 times over'.

The person with the learner-outlook will be the person who lives 100 years, for as Nathan McCall (1994:317) says;

> *Every time I think I've seen it all and experienced all that this life has to offer, I get hit with a new experience that thrusts me into a new reality.*

It appears, then, that McCall has a learner-outlook. He does not expect things to remain the same, *he* does not expect to stay the same. He anticipates that experience will change him. A learner-outlook means being prepared for people and situations to move on.

> *Circumstances can either make of break us. The choice is ours.* (Shwartz, 1998)

In any situation there is a choice; the choice may not be one that is welcome but there will rarely be less than one way out of a situation. A learner-outlook infers that the learner is able to be aware of the choices available and is open to new possibilities. In one sense a learner-outlook means being constantly at the ready, and not allowing complacency about the self to set in and close off potential avenues to learning. It is essentially an attitude and a personal value system that can be supplemented by behaviours and skills.

A framework for developing learner autonomy

There are different ways of thinking about the steps that individuals move up in order to become more effective learners with a lucid learner-outlook. Often these steps may be linked to personality and can be argued from a number of theoretical perspectives about the ways adults learn, which are explored in more detail in Chapter 2.

The following framework is one that currently has some common credence, at least to provide a basic guideline for self-assessment to progress in the area of learner autonomy.

This framework is provided within the 'key skills model'. Within the introduction of S/NVQs a set of key skills, formerly called core skills, has been identified that it is felt everyone needs to succeed in employment, education, training and life in general.

The six key skills are:

1. communication
2. application of numbers
3. use of information
   technology

4. working with others
5. improving learning and performance
6. problem-solving

(QCA:1998)

These skills seem to reiterate the social aspects of learning for life as well as skills required to utilise the resources around you. One we might examine more closely is the skill related to improving learning and performance. The two aspects of this skill relate to:

• identifying targets
• following schedules to meet targets

The skills, as with S/NVQs in general, are presented in developmental stages from Level 1 to Level 5. From the basics of Level 1 individuals are expected to cope with activities of greater scope and depth, requiring more independence in learning and carried out over a longer period of time. QCA sets out the levels as in Table 1.

These descriptions of the different requirements at each level demonstrate a way of understanding how individuals move from a point where lots of support and guidance is needed to being able to plan for and identify the resources needed to achieve the targets they identify for themselves. In other words to move towards taking ever increasing responsibility for controlling one's own learning needs and outcomes.

Depending upon circumstances it is perfectly possible to move up and down the skill levels. It cannot be assumed that once a level of confidence and competence is reached it only moves one way. Indeed a considerable challenge is in sustaining skill levels. Many learning environments may not provide the kinds of opportunities to challenge and develop you within ordinary work routines. Individually, you may need to inject additional resources and motivating factors even to maintain levels of skill of knowledge. This may be because specific skills are no longer required as roles or organisational priorities change. Yet even if it is in the organisation's interest to refocus skill areas it may be in an individual's professional or personal interest to hold on to skills they might want to use again. The same issues can apply to the *learning* skills you acquire and lose. Many factors can

Identify Targets		Follow Schedule to Meet Targets
Can identify long-term targets, and develop short-term measures of progress towards these	⑤	Can analyse the inter-relationship between a wide variety of activities chosen to meet long-term targets and use this information to determine resource needs and draw up a schedule for meeting targets
Can propose, agree and confirm targets, and take responsibility for reviewing these	④	Can choose appropriate activities, and plan and prioritize these to improve learning and performance
Can identify strengths and weaknesses accurately, and relate these to short-term targets	③	Can identify when support is needed and seek feedback from different sources
Can provide information on own preferences, progress of work and work situations, to help in setting short-term targets	②	Can work without close supervision and use feedback to maintain standards and progress
Can provide information, based on appropriate evidence, to help identify strengths and weaknesses. Can check understanding of short-term targets	①	Can follow a work plan (schedule) to meet targets and put support from others to good use

Table 1. Identifying and achieving targets (adapted from QCA, 1998).

serve to rub the edges off critical, reflective practice. Maintaining a focus on personal learning needs and *how* to learn can be blurred by other priorities of the workplace.

Developing and sustaining a learning outlook

The key skill levels presented in the previous section provide a route to bench-marking, that is identifying progressive steps towards individual effectiveness in learning. This in turn acts as a route to enhanced work performance. Using the levels as an individual implies being willing and able to self-assess. Increasingly in today's training and education culture such self-assessment will need to serve different audiences. Fraser (1995:xi) describes the impact of this context:

> As long as recognition of the individual's learning process remains within the heart and mind of the student concerned, we can encourage the journey of discovery and applaud the outcome of increased self-esteem. But when students seek other's acknowledgement of the relevance of their new found learning to, for example, vocational or educational requirements, they must articulate that learning in a manner which will meet the approval of an external reader – and assessor. Private concerns have now become a matter for public adjudication.

This encapsulates the dilemma that an increasing number of work-based learners now have to struggle with. Their learner outlook must be sufficiently vigorous to enable them as individuals to manage the tensions and opportunities inherent in balancing personal learning needs within and outside the learning requirements of others. The significance of the question 'who or what am I learning for?' demands further attention and Chapter 2 will go on to explore in more detail models for workers and organisations negotiating these issues .

Holding on to an effective learner outlook is demanding of your own resources. It is important, therefore, for individuals to seek out opportunities for other support and resources that can help in developing their learner outlook. Many of the subsequent chapters in this book are concerned with identifying and developing a package of resources that will assist in supporting these learning needs, particularly Chapters 3, 4 and 5.

Learning does not exist in a vacuum and learners are reliant upon a range of other resources, from an experience itself to learning support mechanisms, thus enabling learning to happen. Learners should not feel they have to carry their learning needs alone. Nurturing a learner outlook involves the learner in a dynamic engagement with their learning environment and in an active search for resources, human or otherwise, to assist and support their learning.

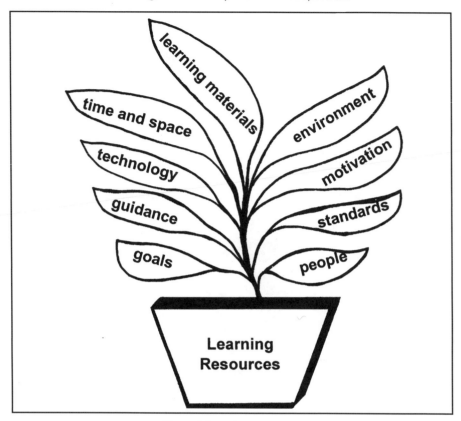

Figure 1. Learning resources.

A successful learning outlook means being able to help your learning to grow with a package of assisted opportunities and resources (Fig. 1).

Part of this building is attitudinal. It implies a mind set that involves focusing on an event in motion and having parallel sets of thoughts at the same time. You may be aware of doing this all the time. As a part of a learner-outlook it includes using one of the strands of thought to focus in on an element arising from a situation and filing it away as a learning aid for immediate or future use. It is, in effect, about opportunism (Fig. 2).

Mike is in a meeting in which the main item for discussion is reviewing a policy concerned with comment and complaint procedures for the services his organisation provides. There are five other people in the meeting. The discussion moves on to issues to do with written promotional materials for the policy.

The diagram below shows the different strands of thought Mike has whilst the discussion is happening.

Figure 2. Multiple thought strands.

He has the immediate needs for addressing the work on revising the policy in focus.

He also considers a more creative response to some of the work.

He then associates this response with additional personal development needs and how he could take steps to attend to them.

He is also juggling other thoughts related to the meeting dynamics and personal life.

So sustenance of a learner-outlook involves ongoing conscious reflexivity of work day activities and shopping around for the resources to feed the changing learning needs that you identify.

Work-based learning and continuing professional development

Developing a learner-outlook is often done within the context of more formal or structured continuing professional development activities.

Reference to lifelong learning has blossomed and is no longer confined in its definition to particular groups in society. As Chapter 2 and Chapter 7 will explore in more detail, there are a number of pressure points acting upon human service professionals to think more strategically about their own professional development.

It is often the case, however, that those in work situations that are career-orientated often need:

clear guidelines, headings, encouragement, even pressure to accept responsibility for their own professional standards. (Gillies, 1992)

In any work situation it is very likely that there will be forces working against personal and professional change. Some of these will be externally driven, whilst others will be internal; perhaps a person's own levels of self-confidence or energy acting negatively upon the need to increase their pace of learning.

Many people benefit from the direction and impetus provided by external motivators to learning. A requirement to update professional skills can feel authoritative, but it can also be a necessary driver to people who may find themselves unable to step off the race of daily working life. If they do *not* come off their pace and energy will of course be drained and gradually fall behind their peers.

Some people are not able to see, however, that if they have a break, rather than falling behind their peers, they may actually be in a better position to keep up or overtake them. Professional development programmes provide one enticement to taking the necessary space to restock energy via new skills and knowledge. The diversification of continuing professional development programmes, and initial professional education and training, has included the expansion of work-based learning opportunities. For many workers this means they need to be able to, in a sense, freeze-frame their workplace activities. They may not actually be able to step out of the race but may be required to create a reflective bubble, whereby they are present at work but also creating a layer of critical distance from what they are doing and observing around them.

In many situations this is desperately demanding of people. There are manifestations of this at all levels of working life; students who are given work loads inappropriate to their student status, senior practitioners who have case loads that need all their energy just to maintain the status quo or volunteers who find themselves performing in a vacuum, empty of support and contextual information. Baptiste sums up the contradictions many workers will experience in being encouraged to sustain their learning when he says:

lifelong learning: a most excellent ethical decoy. (1999:95)

The focus of this book is not to pretend these realities in work place learning environments do not exist. It is to give encouragement and practical strategies for developing a learner outlook within the actual constraints people face in day-to-day situations. It is possible for people to learn creatively and effectively both within and outside the work place. The debates about the relative merits of each learning context will rage indefinitely. Every learning situation's success is determined by a number of factors as discussed earlier. If you do not believe that as an individual you have the potential to affect a significant degree of control in any learning situation you encounter, then this book is probably not for you. Even if you are sceptical of the possibilities for learner autonomy in contemporary human service work settings then you will probably still retain some optimism, simply by the fact that you are still in that field of work. If you believe you can effect change for the people you work with, it is possible you can effect change for yourself.

Summary

This chapter has provided:

- an introduction to the key themes of the book
- a definition of work fit for ideas in subsequent chapters
- an interpretation of an attitude to work within the concept of right livelihood
- a brief outline of what is meant by learning
- an introduction to the concept of a learner outlook that underpins the book
- a discussion of the issues associated with developing a learner outlook and personal control issues in professional development

References

Baptiste, I. (1999) Beyond Lifelong Learning: A Call to Civically Responsible Change, *International Journal of Lifelong Education*, Vol 18 No 2 March – April 1999, pp. 94-102.

Davis, A. (1996 2nd edition) Community Care in Spurgeon, P. Ed. *The New Face of the NHS*, Edinburgh: Churchill Livingstone.

Dwyer, W. (1995) Staying on the Path, Carson, CA: Hay House Incorporated.

Fraser, W. (1995) *Learning from Experience – Empowerment or Incorporation*, London:NIACE.

Gillies, C. (1992) Professional Diaries and Assessment in Bines, H. and Watson, D. *Developing Professional Education*, Buckingham: SRHE/Open University Press.

Horwood, J. (1994) *Caring – How to Cope*, London:HEA.

McCall, N. (1994) *Makes Me Wanna Holler*, New York: Vintage Books.

Phillips, M. (1974) *The Seven Laws of Money*, Menlo Park, California: Word Wheel and Random House.

Qualifications and Curriculum Authority (1998) *Key Skills Levels 1-3; Working with Others, Improving own Learning and Performance*, London: QCA.

Ranade, W. (1993) *A Future for the NHS?* London:Longman.

Reece, B. and Brandt, R. (1996 6th edition) *Effective Human Relations in Organisations*, New York: Houghton Mifflin Company.

Rogers, A. (1992) *Adults Learning for Development*, London: Cassell.

Rogers, C. (1983 2nd edition) *Freedom to Learn for the 80s*, Columbus, Ohio: Bell and Howell.

Shwartz, L. (1998) *New Horizon Coaching Inc.—What's New*, http://www.new-horizon-coaching.com/whatsnew.html.

Sinetar, M. (1987) *Do What You Love . . . the Money Will Follow*, New York: Dell.

Spurgeon, P. (Ed.) (1996 2nd edition) *The New Face of the NHS*, Edinburgh: Churchill Livingstone.

Warner, M.J. (1999) *Enhancing Self-esteem*, New York: Alpha Books.

2. Helpful concepts for adult learning in the workplace

> *Do not believe the person who says 'this is how you do it'.* Anon

No single approach can meet the diverse needs of adults seeking to improve their learning possibilities at work. Individual and organisational norms, values and preferences all impact on how and what is learnt.

For this reason this chapter is positioned before those with a more practical slant. This is to encourage you to approach the 'how to' material with caution, for it opens up *ways* of thinking and doing, not *the way*.

In the following pages some common concepts and issues are highlighted that will offer help in thinking about the messy business of learning at work. Although these span the functional to the holistic, the limited space means it is, inevitably, an introductory approach. Perspectives offered are intended to be illustrative.

Why is theory important?

There are different reasons for highlighting learning theories and issues for those of us who work with people, particularly in a community or social work context. An important one relates to the likelihood that much of our work with people will centre on facilitating change in one or more of the following ways:

- at a personal level
- in terms of social or economic circumstances
- by providing access to practical resources
- at a structural level by campaigning or lobbying to help groups of people

If we work in the business of personal development and social change, albeit in a number of forms, the question may arise:

if we expect those we work with to engage with personal change, should we not be asking the same of ourselves?

Techniques and theories of human development that underpin many group-work and counselling approaches can be seen to be a close relation of teaching and learning methods. Thus there is sometimes a potential for using the self as a model for understanding and acquiring techniques to use with others.

As an aid to making the most of learning opportunities, theoretical insight can also help to expose the process of learning and provide a fresh view on an old situation. With this perspective you may be in a better position to not only engage in change but also to control how and what you learn at work. As Coulshed and Orme (1998:13) say:

> *Theory ultimately provides guidance towards more effective practice, giving a measure of confidence so that workers do not feel totally at the mercy of their working environment.*

Doing without understanding *how* and *why* you are doing it is a worrying way to practice.

Actions speak louder than words

The model of practice learning that represents the ethos promoted in this book is that of action learning. Lindeman (cited in Keregero, 1989:196), sums up the benefits of this for lifelong learning:

> *Learning which is combined with action provides a peculiar and solid enrichment . . . If you happen to be interested in politics don't be satisfied with being a spectator, participate in political action. If you enjoy nature, refuse to be content with the vicarious experience of naturalist, become a naturalist yourself. In all these ways learning becomes an integral part of living until finally the old distinction between life and education disappears. In short, life itself becomes a perpetual experience of learning.*

To situate your learning within work activities creates a need for perspectives on both *how* adults learn and the *contexts* which frame that learning. These are two closely linked entities. As Eraut (1994:19) asserts:

> *professional knowledge cannot be characterised in a manner that is independent of how it is learned and how it is used. It is through looking at the contexts of its acquisition and its use that its essential nature is revealed.*

Learners themselves need to be encouraged to grapple with the context of their learning as a key to understanding what and how they are learning. Thus the next two sections explore the organisational context of work-based learning.

Beware of outcome-driven learning!

Not all opportunities for learning at work may present as controllable by the learner. A seductive feature presented in the current selling of competency-based learning is that it is 'benchmark-driven'. In this context benchmarks are targets to be worked towards that give training providers or employers a standard measurement of performance. In other words a desirable outcome is decided in advance of the learning being undertaken.

This may be good for the organisation or the training provided, but less helpful for the individual's development. People operate within a range of abilities and styles. They also arrive at the targets via a number of different routes. So although the prescribed outcomes may only represent a part of what is learned, they may be the only part that has value to the organisation. There is a chance that other aspects of learning go unrecognised and fade away.

Some people may feel safe and comforted by working to set outcomes. Others may be constantly frustrated at having to fit their experiences to those outcomes. This is representative of the different learning styles people have as well as the varying motivations that fuel learning. Remember: *a* standard is not *the* standard.

The workplace context constantly informs the shaping of your learning as an individual, often in a helpful and positive way but sometimes in a restrictive and limiting way. Your standards may be higher than the minimum the workplace expects and you may feel compromised by aiming lower. It may feel risky, however, to go against the flow of the work routines, and concepts of risk are explored towards the end of this chapter.

The learner within an organisation

The emphasis in the workplace, both in the United Kingdom and globally, is increasingly on the functional. Terms such as 'multi-skilling' and 'transferable skills' reflect the evolution of Charles Handy's portfolio career. No longer can employees expect to stay in the same job or even company for life. This requires a sometimes radical rethinking of your individual place within both the immediate and wider workforce environment.

Waterman et al. (1996) provide a useful analysis of the relationship between employer and employee in this changing employment context. They see a shift in focus from a norm of *employment* to an emphasis on *employability*.

This in turn is presented as an opportunity for development for both employers and the workforce. They see the use of benchmarking and updating as a means of developing what they term a *career-resilient workforce*.

A career-resilient workforce is dedicated to the idea of continuous learning but also stands ready to reinvent itself to keep pace with change. (1996:208)

Constant change is a feature of most professional arenas involving work with people in community and youth work, or the social care sector. There is a need to engage with the nature of a professional identity within new policies, sets of relationships and organisational structures. For example, the emphasis on managerialism and the division between needs assessment and provision of services in health and social care created the role of care manager, and with it a shift in understanding and expectations of the social work role (Coulshed and Orme, 1998, Payne, 1999).

25

Waterman et al.'s model of an adult employee/employer relationship, although drawing its inspiration primarily from the business sector, has resonance for those of us working with people in the voluntary, statutory or private sectors. An outcome of the model is, they claim:

a group of self-reliant workers. . . and a company that can thrive in an era in which the skills needed to remain competitive are changing at a dizzying pace. (1996:208)

Replace the terms *company* by *organisation* and *effective* rather than *competitive,* although this can be an appropriate term in relation to the privatisation of services, and the notion is equally valid.

Crucially the idea of a career-resilient workforce enables a reframing of the context of change from a *problem* to an *opportunity.*

According to Waterman et al. (1996) the key to this reframing includes:

- Ditching traditional notions of loyalty.
- Ensuring employees feel fully committed to the company whilst being a part of it.
- Promoting the flexible employee and removing some of the rigidity in traditional role divisions and skill sets.
- *All* company personnel must be clearly focused upon the purpose and goals of the organisation.
- Employer–employee relationships must shift from parent–child to adult–adult.

These principles have the potential to make a significant impact on the stance of the workplace learner to their learning environment. Learning takes a more central place within the activities and direction of the whole organisation.

It opens up possibilities for potential tensions between the needs of the employer and the employee to be aired and dealt with. Both parties are allowed to have a legitimate stake in training and development activities. The choice between reinvention versus departure becomes a norm rather than indicating a sense of failure on either side or allowing a blame culture to fester.

The model is one that is underpinned by regular assessment of employees' skills, interests and values; constantly benchmarking to identify transferability as well as niche opportunities. A key component is that there are gains on both sides.

Employers cannot guarantee longevity of employment, but a culture of commitment whilst employees are on board is essential. The true learning organisation is one that actually puts the resources and structures in place to support the rhetoric of developing the organisation through its people resources.

In the UK the standard that has been a driver for many organisations is Investors in People. This national award is made to organisations which achieve objectives and continuously improve performance by investing in people. The four principles in the standard are concerned with:

- management commitment
- regular planning
- effective action
- measurement and evaluation

There are a number of other standards that organisations can attain which demonstrate that there is substance behind the rhetoric of the organisation interested in developing best practice through its people. These include 1S09000 and the Charter Mark for the public sector.

In this context a competence discourse makes sense but it can also be a straightjacket. By starting with employer and professional needs, the naming of the requirements to which an expendable workforce must respond is an inevitability. People must fit the named requirements and sometimes this fit is not a comfortable one. Those who can, do, those who can't, leave.

Adult learning in this work-based context is synonymous with key skills. Being able to learn for the purposes of adaptation is a generic skill requisite of the worker needing to succeed in the workplace of shifting functional boundaries. Workers need to be skilled at knowing how and when to share their knowledge and expertise, and organisations need to be adept in drawing out and managing untapped human resources.

Learning often means adaptation for a survivalist function but the truly empowered worker would be someone who could actually influence the definition of the workforce requirements. This requires a balance of personal qualities to use in decision-making forums in which viewpoints and decisions are pushed upwards within the organisation.

Schied et al. (1998) peel away the rhetorical mask within many organisations' espoused commitment to an empowered, flexible workforce based on a culture of trust and equity. They reveal that the expectations of workers to accept increased responsibility for decision-making, customer satisfaction and communication skills, all the while being a team player are really about simple control methods.

They go on to say:

These simple controls were made possible by creating a corporate culture whose values could be internalised by employees, thus internalising control. (1998:161)

Encouraging participation in decision-making is seen as merely another method of improving productivity. At the end of the day power connected to the expendability and control of labour is still within the top echelons of an organisation.

Interestingly, just because the 'production' is concerned with caring work for others does not displace this dominant ethos. The fact that the 'customer satisfaction' element is focused on improving services for those who may be vulnerable or at risk can make the discourse harder to challenge as a worker. Those in work thus frequently find themselves pulled between the requirements of the employer/organisation, their own statutory duties, the service users' needs, their own needs and their vocational motivations.

In this context a learner-outlook can be an aid to strengthen your position to resist the pressure of these external forces. Sustaining a clear learner-outlook may help to identify the opportunistic potential in linking organisational goals to your own. It may also mean being realistic about when these two will diverge and where you wish to invest your learning energy.

Learner motivation

Intrinsic to the success of the career resilient workforce described above is the view that performance will be enhanced by motivational factors, a significant one being the degree to which individual workers feel recognised and valued by the organisation in which or with whom they are working. As Song, Seng and Sock Hwee (1997:2) say:

An effective lifelong learning system for adult learners must respond not only to the dynamic environment but also to the motivational factors.

This section explores ideas about learner motivation as a key inhibitor or catalyst for learning. The organisational issues raised in the previous section are a reminder of why many of us struggle to hold on to our motivation, when the elements of work that motivate us may be dispensed with by changes beyond our control. Ingham (1997:9) has no illusions about the consequence of this on our internal motivators:

When we find ourselves up against it we have to find ways in which to remove or overcome the internal barriers which prevent us from tackling the task in hand; to give ourselves a temporary, even illusory reason for doing it – a carrot by any other name.

So in a change culture at work individual motivators may also shift. Many theorists have grappled with the idea of motivation. The conclusions they reach may be different but there appears to be some consensus that motivation is a complex and perplexing matter. Ideas about motivation today are often based on motivational theories developed in previous decades. Keenan (1995:61) sums up some of the better known theories of

---

Alderfer's ERG theory—states that there are 3 core needs of:
- existence
- relatedness
- growth

Maslow's hierarchy of needs—personal satisfaction needs emerge after functional needs are met, in the following order:
- physiological needs – basic survival needs
- safety and security needs
- social or belongingness needs
- esteem needs
- self-actualisation needs

McClelland's theory—needs are for achievement, power and affiliation.

Vroom's expectancy theory—which states that acting in a certain way depends upon the strength of the expectation of the outcome. So the more positive it seems the more effort will go in.

Herzberg's hygiene theory—that job satisfaction arises from intrinsic factors such as responsibility, recognition and achievement.

---

motivation. Her summary is paraphrased below. The first three theories see generic human needs as key motivators:

Warr and Wall (1975), discuss uses and limitations of well known theories of motivation, including some of the above, with an emphasis on their application in a work-based context. They argue for more attention on people's wants and relatively less on exhibited behaviour. They provide a reminder that:

We may want any number of objectives but once we have made an overall choice this commitment carries with it a kind of traction which draws us along and motivates trial-and-error attempts at sub-goals. (1975:177)

People do not have a single motivation but experience many wants and some are anticipated more strongly than others. The strength of anticipation is influenced by:

- **Arousers**—that increase the strength or a want by, for example, environmental change, encouragement by others and behaviours and habits at work.
- **Constraints**—that lower the want, for example if you perceive a very low (too difficult) or very high (too easy) probability of success.

Kelly (1963) in his work on personal construct theory also discusses theorised distinctions between needs and stimuli. He says that:

. . . in our assumptive structure we do not specify, nor do we imply, that a person seeks 'pleasure', that he has special 'needs', that there are 'rewards' or even that there are 'satisfactions' . . . To our way of thinking there is a continuing movement towards the anticipation of events. (Kelly, 1963:69)

These ideas about motivation can be interpreted differently but for the learner at work they reinforce the following:

- Many factors work to raise and lower feelings of motivation.
- Setting achievable but challenging goals is more likely to lead to success.
- Needs by themselves are unlikely to provide motivation (e.g. someone may need training in lifting and handling as a home carer but want more assistive technology and respite care).
- Social and environmental factors, not just personal drives, influence motivation.
- It is anticipation of outcomes (visioning) that maintains a momentum rather than the reward itself.

Learning styles and preferences

Another factor that influences outcomes of learning is, arguably, the personal learning styles of the individual. There are different views about the degree to which it is possible for individuals to change their personal approach to learning. Increasingly in a flexible learning society, individual learners will be faced with a variety of teaching and learning approaches. So feeling comfortable with different learning styles will be an asset for any learner.

Honey and Humford's categories of learning styles are well known. Honey identifies four ways in which people prefer to learn and uses the analogy of riding a bicycle to describe them:

Activists like to leap on a bike and have a go. They learn by doing.

Reflectors like to think about things before having a go and learn by watching other people try to ride bikes.

Theorists like to understand the theory and have a clear grasp of the concept before having a go.

Pragmatists like to have some practical tips and techniques from someone with experience before having a go.

(Honey, 1998:1)

Schmeck (cited in Gibbs, 1998) identifies two dimensions of a cognitive learning style:

global	analytic
• use intuition and feelings	• focused attention with eye for detail
• more flexible and able to cope with uncertainty	• like order and sequential schemes
• tend to look for patterns through scanning large amounts of data	• use logical thinking and can identify differences in similar experiences

Although these perspectives may help you to identify how you prefer to learn, they should not be viewed as fixed. Honey believes that the learning style impacts on the progress through the learning cycle or spiral. There are different ways of presenting this process. Kolb's experiential learning cycle is a model frequently used to represent learning from experience.

How deeply or effectively you engage with elements in the cycle will be informed by not only your learning style, but also your needs at the time and your motivations. Marton and Saljo (cited in Gibbs, 1999) identify two approaches to learning:

> **deep**—leading to contextualisation and understanding
>
> **surface**—focused upon remembering and repeating

In common with people, situations are rarely identical. Workers need to be able to use previous experience and learn to adapt this to new situations. This suggests the limitations of a surface approach for innovative, best practice.

Beatty et al. (1997:150) have adapted four categories of learning that draw up the distinctions of deep and surface approaches more clearly and is based on earlier work by Saljo.

application	acquisition of knowledge, procedures or skills for use in a practical way.
understanding	sense-making by a personal critique of stored information or knowledge.
seeing something in a different way	new understandings lead to perceptual shifts that go beyond the immediate scope of the material or subject.
personal change	perceptual changes develop into changes in the individual—life and art, as they say, become one.

(Adapted from Beatty et al., 1997)

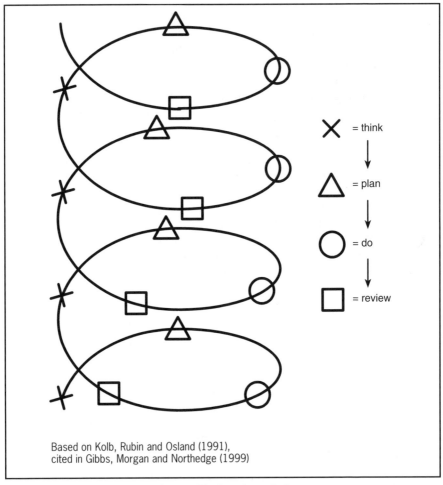

Figure 1. The learning spiral.

Learning at work will involve adopting, at different times and in different circumstances all of these learning categories. It is clear that for the learner working in a change culture a functional, applied approach to learning is more than needed.

Learning as a here and now activity

Having introduced different influences on how and what adults learn, this section looks at the experience of day-by-day learning at work. This represents a shift towards the personal experience of the learning process itself, and upon the immediacy of the work experience and its function as a key learning tool.

There are different ways of framing the notion of learning-in-action or reflexivity including the well-known work of Donald Schön. In a work-based context an appreciation of Gestalt may give individual learners access to a close-up of how to use the 'here and how' to learn.

Some people do not believe in love at first sight. Others will not believe in the possibility of learning through what can be described as 'an immediate moment of insight'; to be in a situation when the immediacy of the action generates new meaning that is instantly recognisable and brings with it sense that you have moved forward irreversibly.

Houston (1982) presents a personal understanding of Gestalt for groupwork that has relevance for conceptualising reflexive learning. She describes a beginning in Gestalt as letting in more or different awareness, which enables us to face the realities we personally constructed, realities that may be a limited and limiting way of dealing with the immensity of the world.

Houston cites some key words in Gestalt as:

Sense. Feel. Imagine. Do. Perceive. Become more aware. (Houston, 1982:4)

The founder of Gestalt therapy is Fritz Perls, and, according to Parsons (1975), he believed that we can become effective learners 'by helping our awareness of what stands out for us in the now'. The emphasis on sense-making, according to Houston (1982) and Lovell (1980), is patterns or systems. The parts that make up the whole in any given moment need to come into focus from which a conclusion about the sum of those parts can be drawn.

In a practice sense this means being intensely and actively aware of all that is going on externally (around you) and internally (in you), and tuning in to what you are doing, feeling and thinking.

It is an observation process in which instead of merely *looking* you are also intuiting. Damon and others have shown, however, that moments of insight are not actually spontaneous but based upon familiarity. In other words practise informs understanding . He suggests that learning seems to be hierarchical.

This links into the notion of learning spirals mentioned in the previous section. Relating this to a work-based context reinforces the need for learners to be open to the process of learning and those moments of key insights.

Sometimes, in trying to convey the significance of the senses with students, they can struggle with the relevance, and they think such concepts are secondary to knowledge acquisition. They are focusing on intellectual rationality as if that alone will provide the key to good learning. The body and self merely gets in the way, rather than appreciating them as a rich site of sense-making. Marton and Saljo (cited in Gibbs, 1999:17), provide a reason for this type of response from their experience:

> . . . *the students who did not get 'the point' failed to do so simply because they were not looking for it.*

In a work-based context many practitioners and students can find it difficult to integrate practice with conscious practising, to push the work issues aside to reveal their own learning agenda. That is, they act and then reflect and analyse what happened and how they performed. This has much value and purpose and ideas for doing this will be given in Chapter 3.

It is equally important that learners can ride the immediacy of their practising wave and to stay aware and in control of both the activities. Rather than saying after an event 'I did x, y and z', a Gestalt approach would mean you say **'I am doing x, y and z now'**.

For work in community and social care contexts this is part of the skills development, of being able to respond effectively and appropriately in unpredictable situations. If you have learned how to tune in to the way your mind and body is responding, you then have the potential to mediate your response. This is an indicator of development.

Hobson and Welbourne (1998), cite Kegan's constructive-developmental framework that describes a process of creative motion for constructing the 'evolving self'. This encompasses a level of learning that is often called 'transformative' (Mezirow, 1997). Hobson and Welbourne (1998:77), go on to warn that:

> . . . *the dissolving and reforming of one's systems of meaning can involve pain and loss, reaching out and letting go.*

Embarking on this level of awareness-raising implies a degree of risk to the learner.

Risk-taking

Risk-taking is not commonly mentioned in connection with learning at work. Experiences show that significant learning often involves elements of risk to the individual. For instance, in the field of outdoor education in the UK, the notion of risk, now set within a regulated safety framework, is well understood. The risk for the individual is largely to be found in exposure to unfamiliar situations in a strange environment. The individual may be required to ask questions of themselves and their actions or reactions in that situation. Such as:

- How will I cope?
- Will I find something new out about myself?
- Will I tap into previously unseen qualities and skills?
- How will I relate to others?
- What are my stress points?

Such unknowns, however, do not need to be confined to another work location. Even in a familiar workplace situation people may put up a number of barriers to taking even low status risks. Wilson (1994:13-22), identifies barriers that stop people taking risks and these are summarised as follows:

Barriers to risk-taking

> **The need to feel secure**
> Many of us fear that if we try something new we may lose security. . . the irony is that this security can change at a moment's notice.
>
> **Fear of failure**
> In trying to avoid failure you may miss the adventure of personal growth, the fun of meeting a new challenge, or the excitement of living for those things in which you believe.
>
> **You doubt your skills**
> The manner in which you mentally talk to yourself impacts on performance. Focus on your strengths and then identify strategies for improving the skills that need developing.
>
> **Changing the way things are done is not easy**
> Change is inevitable. Working with and through change is a source of energy and greater strength.
>
> **Too much to do**
> Often there *are* too many things to do. Fortunately you can prioritise your goals and activities.
>
> (Wilson, 1994)

The first step may be to define the nature of risk as it applies to your learning. What is risky to one person may not be to another. The risk, therefore, may represent an action that feels less safe and the outcome less sure than an alternative course of action. This uncertainty presents challenges for decision-making, especially where different courses of action affect more people than oneself. There will often be ethical considerations in the risk you may be able to take when working with people, particularly those who are vulnerable.

A likely starting place for risk-taking in learning will, then, be an identification of opportunities and situations that present either low-cost risks or a risk that has only personal consequences. Reveans (1982), argues that the most challenging situations are those in which one works on not only a new task but also within an unfamiliar situation.

An example is provided below of such a planning process for risk.

Oona works in a residential unit for learning-disabled adults, and is a keyworker for a young man named Joe. Once a week they walk to the local shops to enable Joe to buy the things he needs, but Oona feels that having done this over several weeks it has now become rather routine for her and, potentially, for Joe. She feels she has developed a trusting relationship with Joe over this time. She also feels she needs to place herself in more challenging situations to extend her skills and that Joe is restricted in choice by the local shops. So she has visited a shopping centre a little further away and identified two ways of getting to the shopping centre for the first visit – by bus or taxi.

She wanted to test and extend her skills and made a list of the possible gains and losses for taking the 2 options for:

- herself
- Joe
- the organisation
- the community

Having assessed the risks and consulted with her manager, she decided that going by bus would provide a new opportunity for extending her work with Joe, and enable her to develop her skills in working with him during and after the trip. She also decided that the bus and the new shops would be demanding of Joe so they would take a taxi on the way back.

In this situation Oona wanted to extend her learning opportunities, but had to put her needs alongside Joe's and those of others. She was able to use her learning needs to enrich the choices available to Joe, rather than staying with the easier but less interesting routine.

When do you want to apply the old saying – you need to speculate to accumulate?

Summary

This chapter has addressed some of the dynamics of the relationship between the individual learner and their working context. It has presented ideas for understanding the personal and social factors that may impact on your learning, ideas you may wish to explore further in other reading. A theoretical foundation has been offered for the practical ideas and activities addressed in the next four chapters.

References

Beatty, E., Dall'Alba and Marton, F. (1997) The Personal Experience of Learning in Higher Education: Changing Views and Enduring Perspectives, in Sutherland, P. (Ed.) *Adult Learning: A Reader*, London: Kogan Page.

Coulshed, V. and Orme, J. (1998 3rd edition) *Social Work Practice—An Introduction*, Basingstoke: Macmillan/BASW.

Damon, W. (1983) *Social and Personality Development*, New York: W.W. Norton & Co. Inc.

Eraut, M. (1994) *Developing Professional Knowledge and Competence*, London: Falmer Press.

Gibbs, G. (1998) *How Students Differ as Learners—581 C7*, Milton Keynes: The Open University.

Gibbs, G., Morgan, A. and Northedge, A. (1999) *How Students Learn*, H581 C6, Milton Keynes: O.U.P.

Handy, C. (1990) *The Age of Unreason*, Boston: Harvard Business School Press.

Hobson, P. and Welbourne, L. (1998) Adult Learning and Transformative Development, *International Journal of Lifelong Education*, Vol 17 No 2, pp. 72-86.

Honey, P. (1998) *What Kind of Learner are You?*, http://www.campaign-for-learning.ord.uk/whatkind.htm.

Houston, G. (1982) *The Red Book of Gestalt*, London: The Rochester Foundation.

Ingham, C. (1997) *101 Ways to Motivate Yourself*, London: Kogan Page.

Keenan, K. (1995) *Management Guide to Motivation*, Horsham: Ravett Books Ltd.

Kelly, G.M. (1963) *A Theory of Personality*, New York: W.W. Norton.

Kerego, J. (1989) Facilitating Learning for Adults through Participation: Some Observations from Tanzania, in Warner Weil, S. and McGill, I. (Eds.) *Making Sense of Experiential Learning*, Buckingham: SSRHE/Open University Press.

Kolb, D.A. (1984) Experiential Learning, New Jersey: Prentice-Hall.

Lovell, B.R. (1980), *Adult Learning*, London: Croom Helm.

Marton, F. and Saljo, R. (1997 2nd edition) Approaches to Learning, in Marton, F., Hounsell, D. and Entwistle, N. (Eds.) *The Experience of Learning*, Edinburgh: Scottish Academic Press.

Mezirow, J. (1997) Cognitive Processes: Contemporary Paradigms of Learning, in Sutherland, P. (Ed.) *Adult Learning: A Reader*, London: Kogan Page.

Parsons, W. (1975) *Gestalt Approaches in Counselling*, New York: Holt, Reinhart & Winston.

Payne, M. (1997 2nd edition) *Modern Social Work Theory*, Basingstoke: McMillan.

Raggatt, P., Edwards, R. and Small, N. (Eds.) (1996) *The Learning Society, Challenges and Trends*, London: Routledge and The Open University.

Reveans, R. (1982) *The Origins and Growth of Action Learning*, London: Chartwell Bratt.

Schied, F., Carter, V., Preston, J. and Howell, S. (1998) Complicity and Control in the Workplace: A Critical Case Study of TQM, Learning and the Management of Knowledge, *International Journal of Lifelong Education*, Vol 17 No 3 May–June 1998, pp. 157–172.

Schmeck, R.R. (1998) Strategies and Styles of Learning, in Schmeck, R.R. *Learning Strategies and Learning Styles*, New York: Plenum Press.

Schon, D. (1983) *Educating the Reflective Practitioner: How Professionals Think in Action*, New York: Basic Books.

Song Seng, L. and Sock Hwee, L. (1997) An Empirical Framework for Implementing Lifelong Learning Systems, http://www.lifelong-learning. org/law,low.htm

Sutherland, P. (Ed.) (1997) *Adult Learning; A Reader*, London: Kogan Page.

Warner Weil, S. and McGill, I. (Eds.) (1989) *Making Sense of Experiential Learning*, Buckingham: SSRHE/Open University Press.

Warr, P. and Wall, T. (1975) *Work and Well-being*, London: Penguin.

Waterman, R.H. Jr., Waterman, J and Collard, B.A. (1996) Towards a Career Resilient Workforce in Raggatt, P., Edwards, R. and Small, N. (Eds.) *The Learning Society, Challenges and Trends*, London: Routledge and The Open University.

Wilson, S.B. (1994) *Goal Setting*, New York: American Management Association, The Worksmart Series.

3. Self-management in learning: issues and tools

> *Not I, nor any one else can travel that road for you. You must travel it for yourself.* Whitman's Song of Myself

This chapter covers ideas for taking a proactive and practical approach to developing your 'learner-outlook'.

The assumption underpinning the ideas in the chapter is that reflective practice requires *practise* and *good organisation*. By using a self-management approach you can become a more effective learner. As Tuijnmam and Van der Kamp (1992) assert:

> *. . . without a positive attitude to education and self-confidence, adults are not likely to actively engage in the lifelong learning society. This underscores the argument that learning to learn is important.*

Why practise learning at work?

Experience with potential social work students in an interview context illustrate the importance of practising learning at work. Many applicants who want to become qualified social workers or similar take up an unqualified post for several years, with the specific intention of applying for a college place on a qualifying course, or they then decide they want to take their career in a new direction.

On paper they present as suitable, yet when interviewed it is clear that they have not *applied* their work experience in any kind of *critical* way. This may show by an inability to relate personal experience to broader issues; or that they present their work experience as if they have been immune to the people or issues that cross their paths on a day-to-day basis. They have taken so many steps yet have hardly begun their journey. It is very hard to convey to rejected applicants that, essentially, they have missed the point of their work experience; that it is so much more than logging up hours or years of experience.

Learning in the workplace should not be promoted as a simpler alternative to using classroom-based training or education. Astley (1992), exposes some of the complexities of practice learning, providing a reminder in his own words of Schon's view that many practitioners may claim 'to embrace the *public* espoused theories of their cultural grouping while actually continuing to practise according to their own criteria'. He goes on to argue that this engenders tensions that need 'exposure and discussion, with the aims of reflection upon and improvements in our practice, and therefore our service to society'.

Learning at work is not a substitute for classroom-based learning. Every format of delivery of education or training has its strengths and limitations.

The experience of assessing S/NVQs, for instance, shows that there are possibilities of unit achievement becoming little more than a bureaucratic exercise in which the notion of development becomes sidelined by the emphasis on recording what a job description might say someone should be doing already.

Whilst there is merit in workers having current skill levels validated, scope may be restricted for enhancing professional development. It is important to have a creative synergy between gaining acknowledgement of existing competence and using this validation as a launch pad for continuing professional development, which is an ongoing process. David Boud in a conference presentation (1998) asserted this position; 'we do not ever **get there** as professionals'.

It is possible for individuals to extend the function of S/NVQs or other similar competence-based learning opportunities to encompass a broader emphasis on personal and professional development. Having to *show what one knows*, rather than just assuming a level of competence has been achieved by virtue of turning up every day, challenges one not to get stagnant and complacent about attendence to personal development.

Steps in the learning process

The remainder of this chapter covers the steps required to learn at work and relates these to a number of practical activities. These are intended to help individuals feel more comfortable in taking more responsibility in their own learning circumstances.

The first step is concerned with ideas on how to *prepare* to learn, something that can get missed in the learning cycle. Planning for learning entails considering the chances and barriers that will impact on how and what one learns. It also means being physically and mentally ready to learn.

It may be the case with many adult student practitioners, especially if they have been away from study for a long time or are only familiar with learning in a classroom-based context, that they may need help with adapting to a significant cultural shift in learning requirements and expectations.

Not only do they need help with adjusting to a new style of learning but they also need to be guided to do this. The exercises and ideas on learning aids are intended to trigger thoughts and promote good practice in what can be called readiness to learn.

The chapter then goes on to outline aids to reflective practice as key components in learning at work. These aids are intended to sharpen a variety of senses that will affect the quality of learning by building confidence in learning *how to learn*. Developing techniques in self-assessment provides a logical supplement to follow this.

It can be helpful to visualise how learning begins and grows. Helping yourself to learning implies engagement with a discrete series of steps. Depending upon your learning needs at a particular time the step you are on will be different. Going up and down a learning ladder will be a feature of lifelong learning in which re-skilling becomes the norm.

Figure 1 shows these steps.

5 Evaluating and moving on—when the time comes to end a learning phase take a critical look back to see what you learnt and how this will help you move on to new challenges

4 Doing and reflecting—while you are doing your work you also need to be reflecting on the situations you are facing. Plus identifying progress against the goals you set

3 Preparing—getting ready to take your learning forward, identifying a personal learning plan, setting up the resources you need

2 Assessing—your skills, limitations, commitment level, type of learning you want to do, matching your learning to personal needs

1 Thinking—about your starting points—getting oriented towards the idea of new learning, making your learner-outlook conscious

Figure 1. Steps to learning by doing.

Readiness to learn

Circumstances in work settings will be unique, irrespective of whether you are an experienced practitioner, coming into an agency new as a volunteer or student, or you are thrust into a new role unwillingly.

A range of contextual issues will impact on the your response to the learning opportunities that are present in the work setting. A consciousness about the nature of work setting may be a help in using it to learn.

There are a number of straightforward ways of raising the levels of awareness of the dynamic between self and the learning context; with the intention of minimising the barriers that stand to get in the way.

Coming to fit the learner role

Another aspect of readiness to learn is concerned with the role of learner, either as an individual or in the role that others may assign to you. The differences in the learning contexts for students and volunteers as compared with qualified practitioners is perhaps most notable in trying to define a role of learner. The seductiveness of being 'the one who knows and the one who does' is a powerful detractor from feeling comfortable with a learner stance.

Social work students undertaking practice placements often find it very difficult to own the role of qualifying learner. A placement should provide and protect a privileged space in which to maintain some critical distance for professional development. It should be a place where systematic reflection and self-assessment carries equal weight to the practising of practice. It is worrying when students misplace a welcoming, inclusive environment as a green light to being 'one of them'.

Whilst their eyes are on the prize of being a social worker they may miss the scenery on the journey. Part of qualifying learning involves acquiring a professional identity that is unique to each individual. In a work setting one has exposure to a wide range of people with their own style and professional persona. As a learner at work there is the chance to observe and mull over these styles and then to make choices about absorbing those aspects you like into a personal public persona.

The focus on competence and achieving the necessary ticks can also detract from taking risks with learning (Waldman, Glover and King, 1999). It requires a certain degree of self-assurance to resist the temptation to become a substitute worker and relax into the role of apprentice. Sometimes, the student cannot achieve this stance by themselves, but are dependant upon the placement supervisors, practice teachers and others in fulfilling their commitment to providing an environment in which the student can *learn* by doing, not just *practise* doing. Placements are precious opportunities as experienced practitioners come to know only too well. Volunteers should also feel that they are provided with an appropriate balance of both giving and receiving services and support.

A learner role for a qualified practitioner takes on a somewhat different emphasis. The employed person has responsibilities and accountability for

Question	Answer
1. What do I want to know?	• *what other services do for and with young people* • *more about the laws that affect the young people I work with*
2. What do I want to be able to do?	• *to develop deeper relationships with young people with whom I work that is more relevant to their needs, not just to the aims of the group* • *do more variety of things with them*
3. Why have I chosen these?	• *if I do these I think I will be working on being a more able youth worker*
4. What should I practise to help me achieve them? How can I act on my intentions? (shown in bold)	• *ask the teenagers what they want to do—**before every planning meeting*** • *observe more actively what is going on and picking up on things earlier—**create a form to help me*** • *speaking up with my ideas to the other leaders more in planning meetings* • *visit other clubs and talk to other youth workers—**1 place every 3 weeks***
5. What might help or get in the way of achieving these things?	• *the fact that I can just pick up the phone and call someone* • *the fact that we do much the same things in the group—this can be a pro and a con—new ideas might be welcome, but some people might not want to be bothered to try new things*
6. What do I know already that may help me?	• *try to use my psychology course to help me analyse interaction between people and to help me do a form for my observations* • *I know the group members well so hope this will help*
7. How will I know when I have achieved or partially reached my goals?	• *set myself some dates to review progress* • *by asking the group members views, asking my colleagues* • *looking at my notes* • *looking at minutes of leader meetings and other records of club activities, e.g. photos*

Figure 2. Jane's specific learning goals sheet.

service delivery that are absent for a student or volunteer, albeit to varying degrees. It can be challenging for a person regarded as competent to practice, to then step back and admit once more to having development needs. A sense of safety in the work environment and management may be a prerequisite to honesty in this regard.

It is interesting to note that in certain management skills audits which I have carried out in companies, it is often members of senior management teams who identify for themselves the most coherent set of development needs. Perhaps this was because they feel in the safest position to do so! It may also, however, be reflective of their appreciation of the need for continuing professional development.

Only you can decide how public to make a self-assessment of development needs and how to address them in the context of the organisation. If you are a part of a learning organisation with an effective appraisal system linked to training needs identification then you are likely to have an outlet for expressing these needs. If you feel you are in a work situation where admitting limitations and mistakes is a sign of weakness then you may have to look outside the organisation for support, though this does not mean you cannot use your workplace to learn.

The emphasis is, however, on determining your own destiny. As Margerison and Smith (1989:100) say: 'the managers who are most likely to succeed make their own route through the organisation'.

Time-management

One of the most common blocks to learning at work is time, or more specifically, people's relationship with time. Whether in a full-time, part-time, sessional or seasonal work it is very likely that most people are juggling with a number of competing pressures from both within and outside the workplace.

It seems to be that it is almost obligatory in arranging diary dates with others that at some point in the conversation a commitment will be qualified by an acknowledgement of too little time. It also appears that not to be, 'busy, busy, busy', implies some form of slacking. A form of competition emerges for activity levels that actually says nothing about quality or efficiency. Wilson (1994:71), cites a quote by R. Alec Mackenzie which summarises this position.

Nothing is easier than being busy and nothing more difficult than being effective.

Here is the key to time management. It means first of all taking an honest and creative look at how time is utilised in terms of output over specific periods. It means asking hard questions that relate to personal and professional goals, both short and long term. The next section shows the stages in setting learning goals.

Time management for the purposes of preparing to learn means creating the space to engage in what learning opportunities are available in the work place and with enough rigor to produce recognisable change in outlook and or professional competence.

Time planning as an aid to initiating change is a highly individualised process that is informed not only by job function and personal commitments but also has to be designed to fit individual approaches to learning, as well as personal time clocks.

Time and task audit

In order to plan for time to reflect and record this learning, it may help to begin by being clear about how you use time already. This might involve going back through a diary or work planner and analysing:

- how your time is used
- peaks and troughs in workload
- daily, weekly, even monthly rhythms in work routines

If a detailed diary of work undertaken is not kept, then record these activities and timings over a period of not less than 2 weeks. If shifts or rotas are worked one may need to adjust the length or period of time that is alotted to the time and task audit.

For each day keep a record of times as well as tasks undertaken.

A time-management issue that may be more difficult to analyse retrospectively is related to personal energy levels, but this can be included in a time and task audit. For example if you notice that you are usually tired at 3 pm on Friday afternoon it makes sense to avoid this as a time to devote to reflective learning. This seems obvious, but planning with awareness of body-clocks and stress points may mitigate against failing to follow through with some learning tasks.

With clearer information you will be in a stronger position to work out an appropriate schedule for fitting in learning-related activities.

SLOT analysis

Another stage of preparation and planning around a personal learning context involves identifying a starting point for building learning opportunities. A practical task to help with this is an adaptation of an old favourite in practice situations. A SWOT (strengths, weaknesses, opportunities and threats) analysis is changed to a SLOT analysis in which weaknesses are redefined as limitations.

This involves taking an overview of the work situation in order to identify factors that will affect your learning. These factors are grouped under headings as shown in Figure 3.

Carrying out this exercise is intended as a first tier of perceiving the work situation as a learning environment. It should start you thinking about the kinds of factors that will have some influence and which, therefore, you need to take advantage of or seek to change.

The exercise should enable you to:

- Situate yourself within the learning environment, that is the work setting.
- Bring into the open the factors you need to take into account in undertaking this learning.
- Begin a process of personal reflection and critical analysis of work activities.
- Provide a record of a beginning to which you can refer.

Strengths

In this situation I have the following qualities that will help me to learn:

  My experience of
  My knowledge of
  My attitude towards

Don't be modest and don't overreach your estimations!

Limitations

I need to be aware of and work to develop:

  The limits of my experience in
  My lack of knowledge about
  My attitude towards

Opportunities

My work setting provides me with the following things to help me learn:

  Resources
  People
  Practice situations
  Policies

Threats

I need to try not to let the following things get in the way of my learning:

  People
  Things to do with my work setting
  Workload factors
  Personal issues
  Other things

Figure 3. SLOT analysis.

Strengths

In this situation I have the following qualities that will help me learn:

My experience of | *doing other Open University courses, managing my time, youth work*

My knowledge of | *issues that affect young people, theory from the psychology course I did last year*

My attitudes | *positive approach to study and self-development like and believe in young people's potential*

Don't be modest and don't over-reach in your estimations!

Limitations

I need to be aware of and work to develop:

The limits of my experience in | *different types of youth work*

My lack of knowledge about | *statutory work with young people, law, girls work*

My attitudes | *trying out new things and not doing the same activities with young people because it's easier. Involving them in deciding what we do each week, getting more facts and not relying on my opinions*

Opportunities

My work setting provides me with the following things to help me learn:

Resources | *don't have very many things—attendance records*

People | *I can talk to the other leaders in planning and clearing up time and check out with them if they thought similar things or differently to me, area secretary has lots of contacts*

Practice situations | *weekly sessions, residentials, when individuals approach me, committee meetings*

Policies | *confidentiality, child protection?*

Threats

I need to try not to let the following things get in the way of my learning:

People | *Robert one of the other leaders who is always moaning about things*

Things to do with my work setting | *staff seem to like doing the same things, can be inflexible*

Workload factors | *this is only very part-time and I can't give as much time as I like, doing the paperwork seems to take up too much time*

Personal issues | *my sister is having a baby soon so I might get distracted!*

Other things | *can I actually do this, I only just passed my other courses?*

Figure 4. Jane's SLOT analysis sheet.

Example:

To provide you with some tips on undertaking an analysis, a fictional example follows:

> Jane is a white woman in her early twenties who has helped run a local youth group for about four years. She is a lone parent bringing up a daughter. She returned to higher education with the Open University and has completed three courses. Her next choice is a social care course that has a strong practice emphasis and will require her to link some assessments to practice situations. She wants to use her experience in youth work to help her, and has seen the course outline.

Jane has done quite a good job at outlining things that will affect her learning. She has also pointed out things that are worthy of attending to in developing her learning goals that may be separate from those of the course. For example, her role in the team and how she can generate more positive vibes if there is someone who has quite a negative outlook. Does she have difficulty in challenging people? It may be that Jane herself cannot yet articulate or answer some of these questions at her starting place in terms of her own awareness, but it is hoped, as she developed her practice concepts, these questions would emerge.

It is important to keep and refer back to the SLOT analysis. Regular reviewing of the original comments allows you the chance to see if any revision of personal strengths or limitations is needed. Or perhaps personnel or policies have changed at work.

This task leads helpfully in to the next issue.

Get organised!

The SLOT analysis as a document for reference immediately raises the need to think about recording and filing. Inevitably, memory alone cannot provide an accurate picture of how you felt some time ago or what the situation was like.

When children grow up it is certain indicators that usually trigger an awareness that growth has occurred—clothes being too small or a change in hair colour. So it is with personal learning, but the nature of that change means that shifts in consciousness and even skills may go undetected because the evidence is not necessarily physical. Again using the child—adult metaphor, relationships with children change incrementally to the point where there may be uncertainty about the memory of how things used to be. Memory can bundle events together into a single thought that is only a partial truth. For example a grandparent might say 'John was a good baby', a phrase that conjures up little sense of the reality of the first year of a life!

Keeping and having access to written records and other artefacts, therefore, is an important part of a learner-outlook. Research for this book used evaluation reports from a personal course from many years ago. It was reassuring to see the recollections of that time and also be surprised by the accounts of others involved in that performance evaluation. I also recalled the significance of their role and contributions in providing a balanced view in my course review.

You can watch yourself grow through these records. They can also be valuable when you feel you are encountering challenging situations, as a reminder of the ways in which you have moved on and changed. If you are feeling stuck or experiencing a dip in confidence it is useful to be reminded of even small shifts in competence. Examples of such records and how they can be used are provided in Chapter 5.

Goal setting

One way of recognising change and maintaining momentum is to utilise goal setting. This is a valuable tool not only for novice workers but also for experienced practitioners who are seeking to reframe their practice to encompass a more overt learning dimension. If you are part of a formal learning programme these goals are likely to emerge directly from the course aims and outcomes.

If informal learning is involved you need to set a personal learning agenda to create a focus and meaning from what is undoubtedly the complex and often messy business that is work. An example of such an agenda is provided further on in this section. Unravelling and identifying genuine learning is aided by having learning goals as a reference point for measurement and comparison.

Part of using the workplace for personal development involves extracting from the hurly burly of day-to-day activities those elements that can help *you*. In social care and youth work we need to be focused continually upon the needs of the people we work with and the ethics and purpose of the organisation. It may seem unfamiliar and even an act of selfishness to turn attention upon oneself. In order to develop practice effectiveness one needs, however, to reframe being *introspective* as being *reflective*.
Functioning on two levels at the same time is needed—as an operator and a learner. Whilst doing, one needs also to be anticipating improvement.

There are lots of things you can learn from each situation which is presented. In order to learn strategically from each opportunity, a purpose and focus helps.

The form below offers a way of identifying personal learning goals for use either as it is, or with some adaptation. Asking questions of yourself and listing your responses is a good way in to the task. Other personal questions will probably arise. In other circumstances, talking to yourself can be considered a bit odd, but, it's all about building that critical dialogue. No one is listening but yourself anyway!

Purposes of the activity:

- to move from the general to the specific in planning individual learning goals
- to bring the notion of self-directed learning from a thought to a deed
- to provide markers by which to measure some forms of progress
- to provide a document that may serve not only a personal function but the basis of a formal assessment (for example an S/NVQ evidence diary)

When setting these learning goals remember the following:

you can miss the target by shooting too high as well as too low. (Alinsky, 1971:xviii)

So make your goals S.M.A.R.T. ones.

- Specific
- Measurable
- Attainable
- Realistic
- Time-bound

SMART objectives is a commonly used idea, originating from Malcolm Knowles the well-known adult educator.

Question	Answer
1. What do I want to know?	
2. What do I want to be able to do?	
3. Why have I chosen these?	
4. What should I practise to help me achieve them? How can I act on my intentions?	
5. What might help or get in the way of achieving these things?	
6. What do I know already that may help me?	
7. How will I know when I have achieved or partially reached my goals?	

Figure 5. Specific learning goals.

Using Jane's example will illustrate how to turn the issues identified in the SLOT form into specific learning goals that are Jane's personal learning agenda.

Mental preparation for learning

In addition to the practical steps described above, successful learning also involves a belief in your own capacity to learn and develop. If people have experienced a lack of success in traditionally defined milestones of schooling or training they may lack confidence in their own abilities to learn. As a worker involved in supporting young people excluded from school states:

> . . . *they almost, therefore, give up before they have started. You have to go step by step so that they actually come to realise they can achieve things.* (Lois, 1997:57)

A positive perspective will enhance the chances of succeeding. Ways of doing this are suggested below.

Visioning

The notion of visioning is used in all sorts of circumstances. When writing this book I needed to use visioning to achieve my goals, and therefore had to imagine the book on a shelf, in someone's hand, as real paper with the title on the front cover. There had to be a perceptual shift relating to where I was and the goal I had set myself. Part of this involved saying to people 'I am writing a book' and of course coping with the scale of the task by taking one step at a time, even if it was one line at a time!

Whatever situation you are in and whatever goals or dreams have been set, try to create a picture of what an end might look like, and then identify stages and actions that might lie along the way. It might be a pay rise, an application for a course, a service user moving into their own home from supported housing. The emphasis is on *an* end, knowing that goals and circumstances can change, and in the learning journey one destination signals the sight of another further down the road.

Focusing

As a complement to the long term vision you may need to prepare mentally for learning by sorting things in both private and working lives that may be taking up a lot of mental energy. If you are undergoing difficult relationship problems in or out of work this may clog up thinking time that you might otherwise have for learning. Trying to do everything may merely create unnecessary pressures and you may set yourself up to fail in your learning goals. Either moderate these goals accordingly or delay your learning plan.

Now you are ready

In this section you have been presented with ideas and activities designed to help you stop and prepare before getting down to the business of learning. If you are to make the most of learning opportunities this means devoting time and effort to preparation. This, as with so many activities, is an important key. If you are considering a formal learning programme, make sure you have explored all the options available. The choice of learning opportunities is expanding and just because one came along that seems appropriate does not mean it is the best one for you. Chapter 7 looks in more detail at the issue of choice and opportunities for learning at work.

Aids to reflective practice

In the previous chapters the significance of reflective practice to learning in the workplace has been promoted, and what follows are some practical tips for developing habits in reflective (after you have done something), and reflexive (whilst you are doing), thinking. The reason for providing such tools is to offer visible hooks to generate and sustain the momentum of learning. The first tangible activity involves making some dedicated space to practise.

The key to nurturing reflective skills is creating the space to reflect, which seems obvious. Yet the main argument expressed by people aiming to learn at work is the problem of not enough time. Of course time and pressures of responsibilities are issues that get in the way. Demands of the work setting, its newness or its intensity; managing continuous change as a practitioner; all these factors can mitigate against prioritising reflective activities. Earlier in the chapter time management was discussed. Everyone should identify some times for reflecting on learning.

The most appropriate analogy in response to time factors is the notion of the five minute workout, so prevalent in television keep-fit slots. The rationale is that everyone can find a few minutes somewhere in the day to tone up and that a few minutes *does* make a difference. The same applies to reflective habits and no sweat is involved! A personal view is that little and often works well in relation to developing critical reflective skills. By developing them as a low key habit they may more easily nestle within the hustle of the working environment. Some people like and need to use routine to fulfil their plans, whilst others find this is anathema. Whatever the case, knowing your personal preferences will help in developing a habit to suit you.

The following sections offer suggestions for how to use the thinking time. First, the need to decide on a good space.

Think about your working day—are there routine features such as lunch or coffee breaks, daily meetings, recording times, periods for telephoning people, start or end times?

Could you identify an activity or period of the day that is conducive to building in a reflective activity?

Possible triggers:

- Stop-the-clock—set yourself an alarm call during the day.
- Mark a time as busy in your diary.
- Use a tape in the car home to talk to yourself.
- Develop a Pavlovian response – perhaps someone else's daily habit such as when they have a coffee break.
- Find an activity rather than a time. Whilst not endorsing taking up smoking, there is the example of a youth work manager who recognised that her slot came when she went outside the building for a cigarette, and had linked the two activities of smoking and reflecting together in a conscious way.

I've found *my* 5 minutes!!

Then hold on to those 5 minutes!

As already mentioned there are likely to be various agendas informing what you learn. As well as a formalised learning programme at work, there may also be personal goals that are complementary. The tools below are designed primarily to help you reflect and learn but may also help with assessment, which is the focus of the next section.

Recording your learning using diaries or learning logs

The use of learning logs or learning diaries is an increasingly common feature of formal education programmes. For the practitioner in the workplace they can provide a vital aid in:

- offloading the baggage of the work day
- developing a critical distance so that events and issues become a catalyst, rather than the blocks that hold back your learning
- providing evidence for assessment

Keeping a regular record of time and action is probably the best known form of recording, but in a learning context there is scope to play with different variations of diary-keeping to suit your own needs and ways of linking thought and experience. A summary of these is shown as Figure 6.

Daily diary

Probably the most common approach is one where thoughts, events and actions are recorded on a daily basis. These generally involve a free hand

Daily diary—keep a free hand account of events at work and write whatever comes in to your head after each session. If you like diaries, great, but people often get bored by them and give up, thus the alternatives below.

Time and motion chart

If you do the same task regularly at work, a helpful way to identifying progress is to watch over a period for reductions in the time it takes to complete the task and how the quality improves. e.g. neater handwriting for end of session reports! Does the terminology become more familiar and easier to understand? Can you get hold of information more easily/quickly?

Critical incident diary

This form of diary-keeping makes the most of events that happen at work and which strike you as very significant; critical to your learning. This does not mean 'critical' as dramatic or awful. It means take a problem-solving approach to a situation and deconstruct a particular incident to analyse what happened. The first question might be why was it a critical incident for *you*? This form of diary will be used regularly but does not need to be daily. It should be driven by your own interest rather than routine.

Personal feedback sheet

Design your own feedback sheet to fill in at the end of a session. This might have questions to your specific learning goals or general items. Once you've done copies of the form it's a quick and easy way of getting into a recording habit. Think about your feelings as well as actions:

were you feeling energetic/sick/fed up/distracted on particular days?

did you feel the same at the end of work as at the beginning?

did something really positive or negative happen?

who were you working with?

After a period you might notice trends, connections between factors.

Project-based approach

Think about linking learning needs to a specific activity on the placement? This integration means dual benefits for you and the organisation. The learning activity becomes more meaningful, other people benefit from your creativity and you have an action record of your achievement. If you have ideas talk them over with your supervisor or manager or link person first.

WARNING!!!!!!

Depending on where you work make sure you're not breaching confidentiality procedures e.g. recording people's names, letting others see your work. If in doubt talk to your supervisor or manager.

Figure 6. Time and action records

approach and as such will not suit everyone or draw out the best material, since what goes in the diary may not be focused upon specific learning needs. Some people also find it difficult to write with nothing to guide them.

Jim's daily feedback sheet

Day 4

What did I find out about the organisation?

They liaise closely with residential homes where users live—information about an assault on one of the users emerged this morning (concern all round).
Outside instructors come in to do things like judo, and trips to bowling, swimming and horse riding often occur.

What did I find out about different staff duties through conversation etc.?

Spoke to Eileen—sports and rec. supervisor. She told me about all they did—everything you could imagine! We went out of centre, by minibus, for a walk.
They co-operate with a farm centre where they go horse riding. Helpers at farm centre also have learning disabilities—good role modelling.
Paul—deals with computers—thinks they could be used more.

How did I feel today?

Much better this morning although it was chaotic first thing. Lots of users had lost their new timetables. I tried to get more involved but still feel a bit useless at times—everyone is so busy.

Other comments

Decided to go on staff trip to the dogs on 10th—staff are really friendly.

Day 15

What did I find out about the organisation?

John and Lee (staff) went to Olympia yesterday for an exhibition on education. Won a competition for free internet access and to have their own web site—very excited and looking forward to using it.

What did I find out about different staff duties through conversation etc.?

Lorna had to sort out a problem with a user who had thrown coffee over someone else. He will be assessed and a psychologist will speak to him about controlling his emotions.

How did I feel about today?

Beginning to take and be given more responsibility. I looked after the key group and ran a session in the absence of instructors, felt like I was getting down to the 'real' thing.

Other comments

I have noticed a lot of people off ill—probably due to exposure to lots of germs and stress. End of week—very tired but feeling good about the work.

Figure 7. Jim's daily feedback sheet.

On the plus side a daily diary can present as straightforward and generate an authentic account of what seemed significant on a particular day.

Personal feedback sheet

For those who find it more difficult to think of what to put down in a diary an alternative is to develop a set of rhetorical questions for the end of each day. These can vary as your needs and perspective changes. An example is provided (Fig. 7) of someone's daily feedback sheet for two different days when on a placement in a day centre for people with learning disabilities.

Time and motion audit

The drive for industrial productivity generated the time and motion study. Production might focus on the number of units a worker could process in a specific period of time and methods for improving the rate of units per hour. Such calculations tie in to resource distribution and output. Clearly the human service practitioner is not simply dealing with units, but there are many tasks associated with jobs that may be functional and repetitive. One way of noticing progress is to use the principles of time and motion studies in those areas of your work which present on a regular basis.

A simple chart can show that whereas an assessment form once took four hours to complete it now only takes two. The shifts can be represented graphically—dots, lines. A writer, for instance, may represent word-count. A good writing period may go from producing 200 words per hour to 400. There is another benefit of noting shifts in the relationship between time and output. *It can alert practitioners to the onset of complacency and drop in standards.* A report taking 40 minutes when once it took two hours maybe a sign that detail and care is missing (Fig. 8).

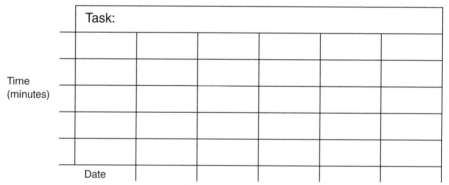

Figure 8. Time and motion audit.

Critical incident diary (CID)

Another form of focused diary keeping is called a critical incident diary. Whilst at work, situations arise that are potentially pivotal in furthering learning. The word 'critical' means key or significant rather than necessarily dramatic, drawn from critical incident analysis. A critical incident does not have to be a crisis or notable in terms of it being out of the ordinary. Rather it may refer to an event, process or situation that opens the door to a number of interesting questions which form the basis of a reflective analysis. By recording in a systematic way incidents which occur you should be able to move from anecdotal recollections to an analysis which has meaning to your own learning development needs. It should also help you to sharpen your reflexivity, that is, the ability to think critically and analytically in the moment an event is happening, an essential skill in work with people. This enables you to recognise an incident as critical and to utilise its learning material by unpicking the specifics of what happened.

How to compile a CID

There is no single way, so adapt a recording mechanism from the model suggested (Fig. 9) to fit your own style.

Have a go at piloting your way of presenting a critical incident. Part of the piloting involves heightening your awareness of the triggers that might make *you* label an incident critical (these will vary from person to person). Remember 'critical' need only to refer to a situation which seems significant in relation to your learning goals and requirements.

Try to identify a time soon after the event when you can reflect in writing and keep it up. Two incidents a week seems reasonable, to gain a benefit from the CID. A CID is a good way of learning from mistakes.

Charting feelings

Awareness of your body's messages helps you stay in touch with responses to situations you encounter. You can use your physicality to monitor and hopefully take charge of those responses. How do you notice that you are:

- nervous
- attentive
- angry
- afraid
- excited
- disturbed
- stressed

What is triggering these feelings and behaviours?

How are they affecting your reactions and actions?

How does being conscious of your feelings help you to manage them more effectively?

Do you notice a change in your reaction to a similar situation?

What do you think this change indicates?

Do you feel stuck in your responses?

Are your emotions your friend or foe or sometimes both?

Does the mood you came to work in affect your performance?

Do the feelings you have at the end of the day go home with you?

Can other people or resources help you to manage your feelings better if you think they are keeping you from being in control?

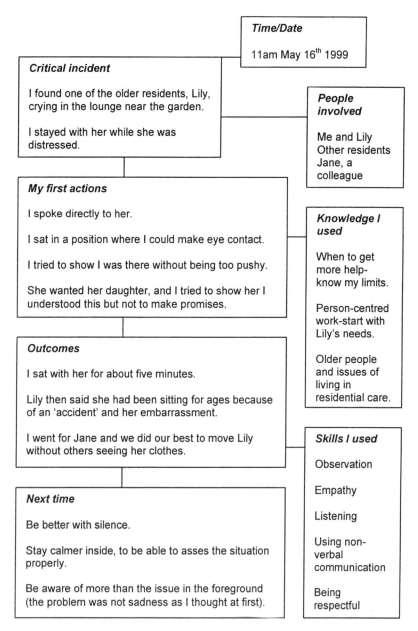

Time/Date

11am May 16th 1999

Critical incident

I found one of the older residents, Lily, crying in the lounge near the garden.

I stayed with her while she was distressed.

People involved

Me and Lily
Other residents
Jane, a colleague

My first actions

I spoke directly to her.

I sat in a position where I could make eye contact.

I tried to show I was there without being too pushy.

She wanted her daughter, and I tried to show her I understood this but not to make promises.

Knowledge I used

When to get more help- know my limits.

Person-centred work-start with Lily's needs.

Older people and issues of living in residential care.

Outcomes

I sat with her for about five minutes.

Lily then said she had been sitting for ages because of an 'accident' and her embarrassment.

I went for Jane and we did our best to move Lily without others seeing her clothes.

Skills I used

Observation

Empathy

Listening

Using non-verbal communication

Being respectful

Next time

Be better with silence.

Stay calmer inside, to be able to asses the situation properly.

Be aware of more than the issue in the foreground (the problem was not sadness as I thought at first).

Figure 9. Critical incident diary – (spidogram layout, but you can choose your own). This example was done by Maggie, a care asistant in an older persons' residential unit.

Don't leave feelings, emotions and senses out of the learning equation. The two examples below show different experiences of the place of emotions in the learning process.

1. Holly is a first year student on a social work qualifying course. She feels that the placement is a piece of cake and feels good about her ability to keep professional distance from her work and not to get involved. In her second year she has a placement which requires her to recommend a decision for a mentally ill person that has significant implications for the life of that person. She finds herself overwhelmed by a range of emotions that last several weeks. These emotions have triggered a significant shift in her understanding of the power and responsibility of social work. Theory, reading and other experience had not given her this insight. Talking through her emotions with her practice teacher and a fellow student she is able to reach a deeper understanding of her professional identity.

2. Morris is a part-time worker for a detached youth work project and is aware that before presenting a monthly report to his management committee his hands sweat, his heartbeat rises and his mouth is very dry. Even though he prepares his report in writing he feels he does not present as effectively at the meeting as he would like. Finally he is able to talk through the problem with his manager and is offered the chance to attend a workshop on public speaking. He practises some of the strategies in his day-to-day work. At the next meeting, although he experiences similar feelings, he tries out three of the strategies he has been practising and feels encouraged by the lessening of the 'symptoms' even as he talks through his report. His tactics include:

- Choosing a friendly face in the room to look at as a way of keeping his head up and eyes forward.
- Writing key words about his report on cards, rather than reading from the report itself.
- Consciously trying to keep his back straight but body relaxed to help his position for breathing.

The next month he is aware that his usual signs are significantly reduced and he concludes that he has learned to manage himself better in meetings by self-awareness, training and practise.

Self-assessment

Morris's example in the previous section shows that self-awareness and self-assessment often go hand in hand. You may be required as part of a learning programme to self-assess your learning and performance. Or if you are involved in self-directed learning you may find that you have to be your own assessor of your learning. Self-assessment is increasingly becoming part of the culture of schooling in the UK and this gives hope for more people being familiar with the challenges and benefits of self-assessment.

There are of course a myriad of techniques, intentions and layers of involvement in self-assessment. The activities included earlier in the chapter incorporated self-assessment. For the busy learner at work a user-friendly form of self-assessment may imply:

- Using limited time and energy, so as not to impinge too much on working activities.
- Relevance to the actual work going on so the connections between learning and practice can be found.
- Evidence that is straightforward to identify, probably from different sources.

Proformas and checklists can be viewed with some resistance and scepticism, perhaps because they do not allow individuals to reflect their personal styles. They may act as a constraint, or represent another expression of bureaucracy and standardisation gone too far.

For the busy person at work, forms can also take the work out of self-assessment. Tick lists probably have as many supporters as detractors. A reason for having the same forms is that they will elicit information of a similar nature. Self-assessment is likely to be an ongoing rather than a one-off process. It needs, therefore, to be centred on checks which look at similar things over a period of time. A proforma or list of questions can help to encourage consistency, at least until the assessment process is familiar. I have not included a single check-list because each learning situation needs a tailored assessment.

If other assessors are judging your assessments, you want to feel assured that the criteria for assesment and presentation of the assessment evidence is as transparent as possible.

In the steps to learning at work shown earlier, the top two were for monitoring and evaluation. Self-assessment implies monitoring your progress and evaluating your performance as well as the tools you used. This review stage is a critical one in the learning cycle. Sometimes this may come sooner than expected, for example if you are not able to continue a course or job for some reason. It is important to acknowledge the closure of a particular stage or learning period, and whether you reach the evaluation stage at the time planned or not.

Remember your SMART goals and make your evaluation specific and focused too.

Evaluating progress during a specific period of time is the end of just one cycle in a lifelong spiral of personal development and change. So if you have not taken as many steps forward as you might have hoped then there is no

The goals I set myself	Progress I have made and how I can show this (evidence)	What helped me get there	What got in my way	New action points

Figure 10. Progress review table.

point on blaming yourself. There is always more time and more opportunities. Of course, on formal learning programmes you may feel that you only get one chance, so build in review points at times that allow for plugging gaps in learning if necessary.

You will probably find you have learned unexpected things. When you start at a place of work, you obviously can't anticipate or know what will happen. So stay open to surprises in yourself as you look back at what has been achieved.

Figure 10 shows one way of summarising progress in relation to learning goals. There are many ways of reviewing progress but every way is likely to involve asking questions of yourself, and the most benefit will be gained by being honest with yourself. This means, inevitably, using practice you felt was below par as a chance to improve.

It helps in evaluating progress to talk through your thoughts and conclusions with other people.

It can be good to get feedback informally from other people in the agency. You are not looking for them to say how wonderful you are, but to give a different perspective on how the work went.

You may want to seek out or use opportunities for a more structured review with:

- peers
- other learning supporters such as mentors, college tutors
- a practice supervisor or manager at your place of work
- service users

You might want to share your learning outcomes with them. You might also want to discuss a more general evaluation of the learning experience as shown below.

Looking back on a learning phase

Was the time commitment I gave appropriate?

Did I actually do what I thought I would be doing?

How was my experience different from what I expected?

Do I think I was more useful to the organisation (or link it to whatever's appropriate to your situation) whilst I was learning?

Did I feel closer to the organisation by the end of this phase?

How could the work setting be more helpful with learning at work?

Did I change my views about the agency or the needs of the service users as a result of this attention to learning?

What did I learn about my own values?

Did it help me with my career plan?

Is learning at work a 'good thing'?

Were there other effects of this period of learning?

Any other questions I can think of.

Figure 11. Learning experience evaluation.

Summary

In this chapter you have been presented with some ideas and activities to help you plan your learning and utilise learning opportunities available to meet your needs. These have been presented within the notion of steps in learning—you may need to take a couple of steps back in order to move forward three. It is not a definitive exploration of ways of tackling thinking, planning and reflecting on learning. Hopefully you may feel more able to build the right path to reach your learning goals.

References

Alinsky, S. (1971) *Rules for Radicals*, New York: Vintage Press.

Astley (1992) Knowledge and Practice, in Bines, H. and Watson, D. *Developing Professional Education*, Buckingham: SRHE and Open University Press.

Bines, H. and Watson, D. (1992) *Developing Professional Education*, Buckingham: SRHE and Open University Press.

Boud, D. (1998) Keynote speech, *SAPHE Conference: Learning to Learn*, July 1998 University of Bristol.

Garratt, D., Roche, J. and Tucker, S. (1997) *Changing Experiences of Youth*, London: Sage Publications.

Margerison, C. and Smith, B. (1989) Shakespeare and Management, *Management Decision*, Volume 27 Number 2, Bradford: MCB University Press.

Tuijnman, A. and Van der Kamp, M (1992) Learning for Life; New Ideas, New Significance, in Tuijnman, A. and Van der Kamp (Eds.) *Learning Across the Lifespan—Theories, Research, Policies*, Oxford: Pergamon Press Ltd.

Tuijnman, A. and Van der Kamp, (Eds.) (1992) *Learning Across the Lifespan – Theories, Research, Policies*, Oxford: Pergamon Press Ltd.

Waldman, J., Glover, N. and King, L. (1999) Readiness to Learn—An Experiential Perspective, *Social Work Education*, Vol. 18:2. 219 – 228.

Wilson, S.B. (1994) *Goal Setting*, New York: American Management Association, The Worksmart Series.

4. Learning supporters

> *Try viewing everyone who comes into your life as someone who can teach you.* Wayne Dwyer

Learning is not a solitary activity. The influence of other people in the workplace informs learning in ways as diverse as people themselves. Often this influence is visible and explicit through the relationship or role a person has. In other circumstances the opportunity to be helped may be more subtle.

Who can help you learn?

This chapter will look at a range of what I call learning supporters. It may help you to take a fresh look at the people around you so that you can make more of your professional and personal networks for learning. If you have identified new learning needs you might want to consider who else can help you meet them.

There are many terms for learning supporters floating around in the workplace that will have different connotations according to the context in which they are used.

Assistance with learning is often provided in ways that are outside a person's formal role, title or remit. For example mentoring might be provided by someone who does not carry the title or responsibility of a mentor. By naming and describing ways of helping, you can decide for yourself what sort of support you have and still need. Reece and Brandt (1996:269) assert that support is not a matter of hierarchy.

> *Everyone in the organisation has opportunities to recognise the accomplishments of others.*

They identify the power of positive reinforcement. For example your sense of a job well done will probably be enhanced if a colleague or manager confirms this view. Being noticed by a senior colleague or manager may boost self-esteem but worthy comments from other sources may be just as valuable, particularly when they are close to the heart of your practice.

It helps to be open not only to the praise, but also the criticism and comment that may arise from anywhere in the workplace. This can promote reflection and learning.

For example, a personal quality that someone working with challenging user groups may value in themselves is an ability to stay immune to the 'flak' they receive. This quality is a limitation if, when hearing what may be very valid criticisms of an aspect of practice or the service, those views are not genuinely listened to. More valuable qualities may be:

- to be able to recognise and act upon areas for self-improvement
- to treat every situation and piece of feedback on its individual merits

As a single learner within a work setting it can be a lonely path to tread if it is not supportive of learning and open dialogue. The politics of the workplace can present a big barrier, and it is naive to picture all work settings as learning organisations. The pace of change, its associated stresses and inflexible cultural norms, can also block learning plans.

If you do not have a named learner role, as with students on practice placements, you may encounter some resistance if you take an independently-initiated learning approach. Attendance on external or off-site courses marks out the learning zone for the learner as well as those around them. With workplace learning there is the potential for boundaries to become blurred.

Part of a potential resistance to colleagues who take control of their own professional development is the way good learning may have a knock-on effect within the workplace. An individual's learning has the potential to disturb the status quo which may either be welcomed or viewed with suspicion.

Even when a group are learning together the individual members of that group will respond uniquely to the learning situations they encounter. In a group of S/NVQ candidates in the workplace, for example, it would be very surprising to find members progressing in a synchronised pattern. Individual understanding of requirements, abilities and opportunities to evidence performance criteria will all influence progress.

So although learning involves others, it can also be a lonely activity and you may need considerable motivation and self-determination to sustain the goals you set yourself. It helps to be able to place a distance between emotions generated by such politics, and view colleagues and others as potential *resources* for working towards learning goals, even if it feels inappropriate to call them *allies* in such an endeavour. You may even transfer your enthusiasm and drive for learning to others along the way.

As an individual learner it is important to be able to reflect upon the contribution supporters make to your development, arising out of exchanges that have both positive and negative elements. If you want to learn from others, this inevitably means staying open to things that might be quite difficult to hear. Again, part of a learner-outlook means being open to those who can offer wise words. Not all such words that hold painful truths may be couched in softened terms. The users of the service you provide may have no motive for preparing an easy path to harsh words. It is recognised that emotional distance is not always easy to sustain, even if there is something valuable to be learned for personal development.

Practice example

A trainee practitioner conveyed the struggle he was experiencing in managing the powerful emotions a service user's angry response had generated within him. Although his assessment of the service user's situation had been endorsed by management he found it difficult to handle some of the implications of his decision, mainly the anger and distress from the service user.

He was encouraged not to disown these feelings or view them as inappropriate. He needed to stay with the struggle that he was experiencing as part of the painful learning process of professional decision-making. He was given acknowledgement that the aftermath of such decisions is a particular challenge, to continue to face and work with the person and that the resolution of his feelings would not be immediate. The service user's response provided a powerful reminder of the need to not become immune to the consequences of decisions that may affect a number of people. The service user accelerated the trainee's learning in:

- reflecting upon and evaluating decisions
- how to use support from seniors and
- how to maintain performance whilst dealing with conflicting emotions

It is hoped that learning, however, will also be informed by positive feelings and outcomes. Learning should also be linked to receiving affirmation of what you do well. This does not simply mean asking people to say nice things about you but trying to understand in specific ways why, for example, an approach or activity worked well on one occasion and not another.

In reality it is understandable if the intensity of work pressures cause ongoing performance evaluation to slip. Policies that inform practice are continually changing, however, and what is effective one year may not meet service standards the following year.

Maintaining a learner outlook means continuously involving others in your learning, people who can provide avenues of feedback and guidance. There are many different models of support provision for learners. Considering these may help you to understand better the sort of support you need at this time and who might be able to fill that support role or roles.

These models encompass relationships that are conducted both in person and at a distance.

Mentoring

The concept of mentoring is centuries old and the term comes from the name of the person in whom Ulysses entrusted his son's education before embarking on his sea journey (Fowler, 1998).

In more recent times mentoring has become associated with a variety of helping contexts. In the UK mentoring was linked with teacher training and the guidance trainee teachers received whilst undertaking their work-based learning in schools. Another model from the USA has focused upon adults providing guidance and role modelling for at-risk youth. For example an inner-city London project linking Afro-Caribbean pupils with adult mentors uses a variety of approaches to motivate and support young people at risk of dropping out of or underachieving within the school system (Swanton and Henshaw, 1998). The founder of another mentoring scheme for at-risk youth in Utah is quoted as saying that youngsters are given a 'window on the world'. (Village Project, 1997).

A key aspect of the mentoring relationship is its overt personal dimension. A mentor is generally someone with more experience and knowledge, perhaps also with access to resources, in the areas the mentee wishes to develop further. Mentors may:

> . . . *advise, coach, counsel, teach and model successful behaviours. These roles vary, depending on the abilities of the mentor and the needs of the mentee.*
> (Mentor 2000, 1998)

At work, mentees' needs are likely to be focused upon career and professional development. A helpful way of describing the particular sort of 'wisdom' that is required in this circumstance comes from Reece and Brandt (1996:104). They describe mentors as:

> *People who have been where you want to go in your career and who are willing to act as your guide and friend.*

So the mentor is someone who can empathise with the mentee because they have relevant personal experience to draw on. This is the foundation for relating to their mentee's situation. (Other terms for mentee are protégé, novice or intern.)

The mentoring process can assist both the mentor and mentee in their professional development.

The mentor is required to think in explicit ways about the nature of the wisdom they are perceived to hold and how to use it in an ethical way on behalf of another person.

It is likely that the mentor will have a great deal of taken for granted knowledge. Recognising, articulating and using this in a manner that makes sense to someone else can be a learning process in itself. A challenge for a mentor may be:

- Having to make explicit what they know, and how their knowledge, skills and understanding were acquired.
- Contextualising expertise so that it is relevant to the mentee's situation.
- Using interpersonal skills to develop a relationship with the mentee in which trust and credibility can be the building blocks for mutual gain.
- Being able to empathise with the mentee by being aware of current trends and issues facing people on different rungs of the career ladder.

A good mentor needs to resist imposing their own route on to the mentee's learning journey. In many situations with the mentee the mentor needs to be able to provide subtle triggers and thoughts to enable the mentee to reach a decision or view that is 'theirs', rather than merely mimicking the mentor's views and actions. Clearly there is the potential in role-modelling situations for a protégé to become dependent either emotionally and/or physically on the mentor's support. As in all such relationships both the boundaries of roles and the purpose of the union need to be addressed to ensure both parties' expectations are clear.

Key features of many mentoring relationships:

- non-heirarchical
- do not involve the mentor making judgements about the mentee for formal or informal assessments—they usually provide additional and separate support
- intimate and concerned with the whole person rather than functionally focused
- based on a mutually agreed arrangement for working together
- led by the needs of the mentee

Mentors may be helpful for individuals who have specific learning needs and/or who need special support, for instance, at-risk young people. Other minority or disadvantaged groups and individuals can benefit from a mentor: for example, women in management, black and ethnic minority students, employees with disabilities, isolated carers. Mentors will be people who understand, have faced and found strategies for overcoming the social and personal factors that may hinder learning.

Coaching

A common sight in offices today is someone bent over the shoulder of another colleague who is sitting at a personal computer. Both people are intent on resolving a problem of how to carry out a programme function. Very often this will be an example of coaching in action in the workplace. Not formalised, not labelled, just spontaneous.

Coaching is often about the transfer of discrete areas of skills and associated knowledge from one person to another. In work settings there is likely to be a wealth of diverse pockets of expertise. Work-based coaching can provide a way of keeping a flow of skills sharing going, a flow that should not be restricted by hierarchy.

Coaching is an example of a term that has gathered momentum as a buzz word for motivational training and life coaching. For example, a world wide web site of coach Lee Shwartz (1999) sells his approach to learning and winning.

The coach is a person who sets someone 'on the right track' and helps to keep them there. Raine cites one example of using coaching within a company:

coaching ensures that learning from initial training is applied consistently in the workplace. (1998:16)

Coaching is a one-to-one relationship that may be framed within a formalised agreement in which the coach may be paid or not. Or it may arise more informally, as in the example of resolving the computer problem. Relatively few people may have access to the luxury of one-to-one paid professional support. It helps to be astute in identifying those individuals around you from whom you can pick up new skills, understandings and approaches.

Some common features of coaching:

- task-focused
- generally short term
- concerned with discrete instructional activities
- structured—so that the session is appropriately focused
- regular
- focused upon addressing the question of 'how to do something' or how to do it differently and more effectively
- should involve a mutually agreed written or verbal contract to ensure both parties are clear about both the input and the result of the relationship

---

Coaching is concerned with current tasks and if used successfully can provide a release for creative potential and act as a catalyst for learner motivation linked to self-confidence. Leigh (1995) cautions that the concept of coaching needs nurturing in both potential coaches and the culture of the work setting to be given and received in a way that enhances learning and performance.

Shadowing

Shadowing involves someone carrying out a work related task that is observed by someone with less experience, skill or knowledge who intends to carry out the same task or activity at a later date. Or this situation is reversed with the less experienced person shadowed by the 'expert'.

Shadowing is generally understood to be an observational activity that is, as the name suggests, silent. The person doing the shadowing has no overt role in the work activity and maintains a position close enough to 'the action' to be able to witness effectively what the more experienced person is doing.

The shadow can never truly be an invisible entity. To be successful, shadowing needs to be conducted in an ethical manner, sensitive to the needs of the people with whom the shadowed person is working. It also needs to be well planned. Simply saying 'tag along with me' is unlikely to be rewarded with a rich learning experience. The person shadowing may gain in a voyeuristic sense from the experience but both parties have an obligation to service users to use the experience as sensitively and in as well-managed way as possible.

Shadowing involves:

- Sharing expectations before the shadowing visit.
- Asking what the shadow hopes to gain from the visit.
- Clarifying what the person being shadowed feels they are offering and what aspects of their practice they think the shadow should be observing in particular.
- Recording—considering what methods to be appropriate in the shadowing situation.
- Seeking the approval of any service users for an additional person to be present.
- Being explicit about the role that the shadow will take whilst shadowing.
- Considering and planning the debriefing for after the shadowing visit (options of verbal or written feedback should be discussed).

Shadowing can be intimidating for the person being shadowed. It can also offer a rich opportunity for learning. The shadow may well ask questions and offer comments on observed incidents and behaviours. The shadow may be inexperienced in the situation but not in their observation skills. They may well have insightful comments from which the more experienced person being shadowed can gain. A debriefing session is essential to air and clarify interpretations of the things that were observed.

The shadow needs to be able to relate their observations and actions to their own stance and style of practice. They need to consider how they might incorporate what they saw into their own practice, given the individualised learning context. Perhaps there are aspects of the practice they observed that they wish to reject. Again, shadowing does not infer copying and repeating what was observed. It means witnessing a piece of practice that can be deconstructed. Some, probably not all, of the constituent parts can then be adapted for use on another occasion.

The skills and techniques of shadowing can be utilised for observing interactions between and with others in day-to-day situations. This suggests the need for learners to be opportunistic in attending closely to activities and processes—learning from the actions of others but not necessarily in structured situations as with shadowing.

Role-modelling

Shadowing implies a hope of witnessing good practice, role-modelling is more upbeat and explicit about seeing this in action.

Role-modelling is concerned with one individual tuning in to the practice of someone else and being inspired, encouraged or enabled to progress in the same direction as the role model.

Role models can rarely be assigned, such a distinction is likely to be conferred on one individual from another. Identifying someone else as a role-model is not dependent upon intimacy, personal contact or a discrete or readily defined set of characteristics. A role-model often embodies the possibilities we believe ourselves to have, and who presents the characteristics, behaviours or attitudes we aspire to. The emergence of a role-model may often be about timing. Somebody presents at a particular time in a certain way when consciously or unconsciously we are searching for a focus, trigger or direction for a particular set of needs. Role-models can provide at best the inspiration and more pragmatically the motivation to press on with professional development.

Learning from role-models may arise from:
- observing
- co-working
- shadowing
- experiencing their work second-hand – for example by video

The person may be someone you work with either day-to-day or occasionally, or someone whose qualities have emerged from secondary sources. Of course there is always the danger in putting someone on a pedestal that:

- sets your hopes too high, so that you feel you have failed if you do not reach their standard
- the role-model lets you down
- you become blinkered to other purveyors of good practice

Admire and aspire, but keep a balanced view too.

Twinning

Whilst perhaps not politically correct, this terminology sums up a particular type of individual peer support. The premise behind twinning is to find a match with a colleague with similar levels of responsibility and status and to bring the two people together for mutual assistance with their professional development. Coles (1998:28), cites the example of a human resource director with Nestlé.

Our manager was very experienced in managing brands. The NatWest manager has lots of experience in strategic planning. They ran the process themselves and helped one another with development goals. They found it immensely valuable. The only cost was time and travel.

Key features of a twinning activity are:
- careful matching of the twins
- mutual professional respect
- the need for openness and trust in the twinning relationship
- the autonomy of the twinned pair to develop their own learning needs and action plan
- the bringing together of people from different working cultures and contexts
- sharing of skills, expertise and experience in joint interest or functional areas
- exposure to alternative approaches for tackling work-related issues and for these to be an opportunity for critical dialogue

---

Another type of twinning may be cross-sectoral, for example linking voluntary sector professionals with business leaders (Ramrayka, 1998). The business and organisational benefits in sharing concepts, good practice and options for tackling similar issues in different contexts are matched by the personal gains of the participants.

Activities and processes within a twinned relationship vary but may typically include:

- visits to the twin's organisations
- time on site witnessing day-to-day practices
- time together for mutual discussion (this could be in person or on-line)
- problem-solving of an issue of mutual concern leading to a shared or parallel response

Line management or supervisory support

Line managers or supervisors, if you have them, are likely to be key people with the potential to influence your learning significantly. As Coles (1998:7–28) cites:

All managers have responsibility for development; it is not just up to human resources people.

You will encounter a variety of informal and formalised learning activities and opportunities with your manager or supervisor. These may include:

- training needs analysis
- performance review
- goal and/or target setting—for example how many people you work with (outputs) and what kind of work you do with them (outcomes)
- discussion about particular practice situations
- opportunistic feedback

These opportunities may arise in:

- supervision sessions
- at performance appraisals or reviews
- in team meetings
- in day-to-day work situations

A supervisor or manager may take up different roles to fulfil different tasks in these settings. They may be:

Role	Focus
a coach	training
a critical friend	motivation and tactics for improvement
a counsellor	listening
a disciplinarian	dealing with poor performance
a negotiator	mediating workers' needs with others or vice versa
a link in a chain of command	ensuring organisational needs are delivered
an appraiser	assessing
a supervisor	practice analysis

These roles present the learner and manager with a variety of openings for encouraging the cyclic approach to learning as discussed in Chapter 2—planning, doing and reviewing.

The various roles that a manager or supervisor adopts will be dependant upon a number of factors. A critical one is likely to be how much they are aware of, and use, the pivotal power that their status bestows on them. In relation to work and learning this power can be used for both positive and negative outcomes.

The function of performance appraisal will be looked at in more detail in order to highlight some of the tensions and possibilities for managers supporting learning. Performance appraisal is also a function that may be carried out by someone else in the organisation.

Issues of power are one of the contributing factors in the rocky history of performance appraisal (Hunt, 1986). Despite this background it now seems, that many organisations are situating a performance appraisal system as an integral part of a top-down strategy to link improved motivation with staff development and organisational goals.

Hope and Pickles (1995:6), identify ways in which appraisal may help with personal or professional development. Performance assessment can enable people to:

- Identify learning from past successes and failures.
- Identify areas of work they can improve on.
- Plan ways of improving their support, knowledge and skills through training etc.
- Identify personal goals and steps to get there.

Hunt (1986) encourages the separation of appraisal linked to performance review from discussion of training needs as the former is linked to organisational needs and the latter to personal needs. Although these two sets of needs overlap, he believes one procedure compromises the outcomes of both. Hope and Pickles (1995:76) identify other inhibitors for maximising the learning potential. These have been adapted below:

- subjective bias—the appraiser is too critical or not critical enough
- lack of preparation—by both appraiser and appraisee
- poor guidance from the organisation on appraisal process and criteria
- bureaucracy detracts from dialogue
- poor interpersonal skills and/or relationship between the two people

Arguably these barriers are ones that can be overcome. There are other ways of mitigating against the impact of bias and personal subjectivity in the appraisal process. One of these involves widening the appraisal process to include other people and two way feedback rather than one way from the appraiser to the appraisee. A well-known model for doing this that has also attracted controversy is called 360-degree feedback (Reece and Brandt, 1996).

It involves a feedback loop between an employee, their colleagues and supervisor or manager. Feedback is given and received by all parties. Once again a transparent structure, process and criteria is essential to stop people simply offloading negative feelings and generating a mass of ill-connecting information.

On the plus side it can usefully provide a more rounded view for the assessment which may assist individuals in seeing themselves as others see them. This rounded view is represented in Johari's window which encourages you to request and receive feedback to aid development, from any learning supporter, not just within the appraisal process. The bigger the first window the more open your communication channels will be and the more self-aware you can become.

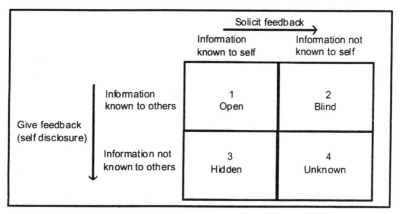

Adapted from Group Processes: An Introduction to Group Dynamics. Third edition. Copyright © 1984 by Joseph Luft. Reprinted by permission of Mayfield Publishing Co.

Figure 1. Johari's window—developing a learner-outlook.

This awareness should extend to taking more responsibility for using supervision. As Morrison (cited in Thompson, 1999:19) says:

Nurse, psychologist, doctors . . . are all much more socialised in taking responsibility for their own learning and development compared to social workers . . . social workers do need to be much more proactive in their own supervision.

If you are part of a formal work-based learning programme you probably have an assessor too. You may feel that the assessor is not there to support your learning but only to act in judgement. Yet in many situations the role of guide and supervisor is entwined with an assessment function, as with practice teachers working with Diploma in Social Work students (CCETSW,

1996). Taylor (1999) identifies the problems of mismatch between reflection and assessment. She says:

> . . . *expecting students to publicly reflect on their uncertainties in a situation where they will be assessed requires a major cultural shift.* (1999:176-177)

Similarly S/NVQ assessors are often line managers or supervisors and the potential problems highlighted in the previous section on appraisal may be present. Pritchard (1995) identifies the importance of differentiating between practice teaching and supervision. Waldman, Dominelli and Borrill (1997) identify three structural facets for supporting successful practice assessment:

- Coherence, clarity and rigor in policies, procedures and regulations framing the assessment function.
- Open communication with clear delineation of responsibilities between key players in the assessment process, not just the assessor and person being assessed.
- Professional development and support for assessors.

These structural facets will help consistency of assessment standards, but it is likely that the use of the assessment relationship for learning, by both parties, will be teased out in the systematic interrelationship between assessor and assessed and the other staff and service users with whom they are involved (Hildebrand, 1995).

The assessor who is also a guide may feel that if their learner fails, it is their failure too. These sensitive dynamics of providing appropriate learning support, whilst also making judgements about that learning and performance have, in other situations, led to a separation of the two functions, as in the Advanced Award in Social Work.

There may be assessment situations where you may wish to look elsewhere, to an individual or a group of people, and with whom it is safer to expose those aspects of your learning with which you are struggling.

Learning in groups

The foregoing, then, has outlined some approaches to one-to-one relationships for facilitating learning. There are also learning opportunities involving groups of people. There are pros and cons to any type of learning activity. For many people the stimulation provided by interaction with a group of people is what makes their learning enjoyable, possibly even fun. Conversely, a group learning experience can dilute the possibilities for meeting individual learning needs because these have to be accommodated within those of the other group members.

Unstructured groups can feel too informal, and when work and learning time is precious, your preference for example, may be for a coaching situation in which you are the sole focus of attention. It is not possible to describe every manifestation of a learning group, partly because by their very nature groups are unique. Below are some options for learning in a group context which may be suitable and apt for an individual workplace situation. Group, in this context, means a collective learning situation that is not contingent upon people being in the same room together at the same time.

Peer and group support

Peer and group support can undoubtedly be a key learning mechanism for both novice and experienced practitioners (O'Brien and Hart, 1999, also citing Pask, 1976 and Jaques, 1985). It can emerge in a work-based context from a number of sources including:

- involvement with:
  –Trade Unions
  –professional associations or bodies
  –specialist practice or management forums
  –contact at conferences
  –internal working parties, for example, concerned with policy
  development or quality assurance
- structured peer-learning opportunities
- action-learning sets
- problem-solving groups

Historically unions have provided a wide range of learning support from lobbying for training to direct work. Payne (1999), for example, describes a new initiative of the TUC's Learning Services, in training members to act as learning representatives, to provide guidance and support to members in widening access to continuing training and education and employability.

Not all of the opportunities described above will happen at every place of work. To learn better at work sometimes means leaving the workplace for a while. A preoccupation with our own orbit of attention can become introspective.

Time out can provide the necessary breath of fresh air to enable the workplace learning opportunities to be used more effectively.

On-line learning networks

Electronic communication has and is widening opportunities for shared learning between those involved in the caring and youth and community services. Dialogue and contact is not constrained by the need to leave the workplace, a problem for workers experiencing a range of pressures restricting their chances of off-site networking.

The Internet and e-mail, in addition to providing an information resource, offer different interactive possibilities for sharing and learning from others.

Participation does not necessarily lead to learning but the opportunities are certainly there for people to take advantage of. Some examples are outlined below:

Electronic newsgroups

On the world wide web many sites will offer you the opportunity to subscribe to a newsgroup, usually by completing an on-screen submission form. In general, these are free and provide daily, weekly or monthly updates on items of news, research updates, links to other useful web sites and editorial views and comments. For example YouthOrg UK, 'The Youth Internet Project', provides a monthly newsletter and is sent to over 500 youth organisations and individuals throughout the UK.

These can provide a time saving and low cost way of keeping up to date on subject specific issues, though, as with many world wide web resources, you may not always be assured of their reliability or credibility.

Electronic chat rooms or conferences

Here is a definition of an chat room taken from an internet site:

Chat rooms are meeting places on the Internet in which you can exchange text messages in real time with other people in the room. This activity, which takes place entirely through your computer, is called a chat session, and is a lot like a conference call, except you are writing messages instead of speaking them.

Each member in the chat session can watch the chat without joining it, or can join the conversation at any time. A chat session may have one or more hosts. The host facilitates the conversation and steers the topic and flow of the conversation. Other chat sessions are open discussions not moderated by a host. (MSN, 1999)

Public chat rooms can be a frustrating experience because they may involve banter which is unfocused. It is pot luck whether someone with useful things to say, who may come from anywhere the globe, happens to log on to the site at the time as you. Public chat rooms on the Internet can be like hanging around in a train station waiting room and chancing upon a stimulating conversation while you are there. For some people it is the unpredictability that provides the buzz, but for the pressured practitioner they may feel it is too much of a gamble with time to warrant bothering with.

Organised on-line conference discussions are more likely to yield focused and worthwhile discussion. The format requires some getting used to for the first few times.

Electronic discussion lists

Electronic discussion lists are rather like chat rooms. The key differences are that you are not logged on at the same time as the other people in the discussion so you can read and respond to the dialogue on screen at your will. This allows for more selectivity in scanning and joining in conversations but lacks the spontaneity and immediacy of chat rooms. There will have often been different strands of discussions going on that you can link in to, depending upon your area of interest. If the discussions come through your main e-mail address, you may find yourself receiving more strands of topical discussion than you can deal with. For example, there is a social work list convened by the National Institute for Social Work that allows for a useful exchange of professional ideas and information.

One of the exciting possibilities in electronic communication is the way it can take you to the work and views of colleagues, peers and others from all over the world.

Video conferencing

This again involves real time dialogue with people linked by video cameras to computers. You may have a one-to-one discussion using a personal computer screen or be with a group of people watching and listening to the other person or people on a larger screen. For many people access to this facility will be limited and it is more likely to be part of a formal programme of learning. The advantages are that people do not have to be in the same room to talk to each other. A telephone conference uses a similar principle but with only an audio facility.

Electronic communication may be via different media but many of the individual helping relationships described earlier in the chapter may be conducted through these media. The differences are arguably in the collectivity of the communication channels. The picture differs considerably from traditional in-person networks in:

- the number of people with whom you can have contact
- their geographical diversity
- the immediacy of the contact
- the choice of contacts
- the different modes of exchanging views, ideas and information, for example the emerging etiquette and style of communication which can be more informal and unguarded than face-to-face situations
- the self-management of using public and closed channels
- the silence of those who are excluded from these local and global exchanges

The potential benefits are clear but beware of the pitfalls.

Learning with and from service users

A key component in successful work-based learning arises from the relationship with service users or customers. That relationship and the activities associated with it is often at the heart of the learning experience.

Practice-learning is largely focused upon improving skills and approaches for working effectively with people. To leave service users out of the learning equation, therefore, seems quite unthinkable.

To consider service users as one group of learning supporters requires a shift in perspective about those who are assigned a role as 'teacher or guide'. A critical aspect of work-based learning, as distinct from learning in an academic setting, where the role of giver and receiver of knowledge is largely institutionalised, is the blurring of boundaries between the person who knows and the person who learns. In the workplace these roles often shift, so that one may be either the knowing person, or a person who needs to know. Harding and Oldman reinforce this view:

> *The split between service users and carers and professionals is in many ways a false one. Service users are also people who have a variety of skills and life experience and live in a world beyond 'services' . . . commonality of experience is a strength, helping to get beyond the divisive 'labels' of particular roles, and it is helpful to recognise it openly.* (1995:5)

A key part of success in being able to work creatively within this shifting paradigm is the ability to feel comfortable with the stance of learner. This theme of the learner role links to the previous chapter's discussion of ongoing self-assessment.

The notion of mutuality is helpful for framing these shifting relation – ships and roles. The question it raises is how an interaction or encounter can have benefits for all parties. An arrogant individual stance in a working relationship will negate the potential for the helped to also be the helper.

Clearly this form of dialogue owes much to the ideas of people like Gerard Egan and Carl Rogers. Fashions fluctuate, but the underpinning notions of respect and mutual regard surely have as much relevance today, when the practitioner is required to work in ways that offer the potential for service users to empower themselves.

It seems entirely appropriate that methods of learning should be underpinned by values that are in harmony with the way you wish to practice. Involving service users as givers as well as receivers in the learning paradigm is a credible way of doing this.

There is a continuum of roles that service users may have in a helping relationship. Circumstances and the needs and abilities of service users or learners will affect the roles adopted.

service users as vessels for for trying things out	_____	service users design and assess learning programmes

The roles are as much about attitude as activity. The views of service users on training for community care, presented in a report by the Social Services Inspectorate (1994), provide a summary of attributes workers should demonstrate:

- develop personal awareness
- understand the abilities and disabilities of service users
- be honest
- treat people as individuals
- establish and maintain two-way communication channels

With these qualities, workers as learners will be in a stronger position to learn from service users in a manner that expresses respect, recognises the autonomy of the individual and demonstrates partnership principles.

Service users may fulfil nearly all of the supportive roles discussed earlier. Of course, there are many complex and varied issues for involving different service user groups in some activities, including formal assessment of learning (Waldman and Tuson, 1997, Beresford, 1994, Trevillion and Beresford, 1996). Barriers to this level of participation should not be a deterrent to other types and levels of activity. Also, involvement in assessment should not be seen as the gold standard because it may not represent service users' priorities and preferred involvement.

Defining personal learning networks

Having addressed the types of helping roles and actions that can enable you to learn from and with others, we look at further ways of thinking in more detail about the actual people you know who may form part of 'the learning web'.

Learning stream exercise

It may be useful to first of all step back and trace your professional development with any significant people who helped you on the way, directly or indirectly.

This can be represented by a stream that is analogous for the continuous flow that is learning. It typifies the meanders and eddies that can take us in new directions and cause turbulence. It can also reveal some unexpected and surprising sources of help over a period of time.

If your career has been a long one or involved a number of pathways you might choose:

- A phase that is very special to you.
- One area of the work you do; perhaps your remit has changed to encompass a new role that took you on a new learning curve.

- How you have been helped by a specific group of people (e.g. line managers, colleagues, service users or trainers/educators).

Are there people and periods that represent the following?

Rapids = accelerated learning

Waterfall = crisis-driven learning

Boulders = blocks to learning you had to navigate

Fork = different learning going on in tandem

Secondary stream = a diversion that brought you back to the main stream (e.g. a course)

Straight and flowing = steady learning phase

Pool = watch for complacency

Get the idea?

A little practice will clarify the idea (see Fig. 2).

Example—health care professional

- When you look at your stream are you surprised by your visual journey?
- Has your learning been driven by mainly positive or negative encounters?
- Has it involved rapid progress or did you encounter lots of slow moving pools along the way?
- Would you like your stream to flow differently in the future?

If yes, can you do with some more 'waterway management' to help?

Learning web exercise

Then and now

Your past stream may have helped you to identify the best kinds of learning encounters or relationships to suit your style of learning. The next exercise is designed to help you identify learning supporters for the immediate or short term future.

Who do you have around you now who can fast-track your learning in the direction *you* want it to go?

To help you think about this, Figure 3 invites you to fill in your own learning web.

The purpose of a learning web is to:

- bring into focus the human learning resources around you
- identify ways in which individuals and groups will support your learning
- help you to expand your options for getting the help you need to learn
- aid reflection on developing your learning style

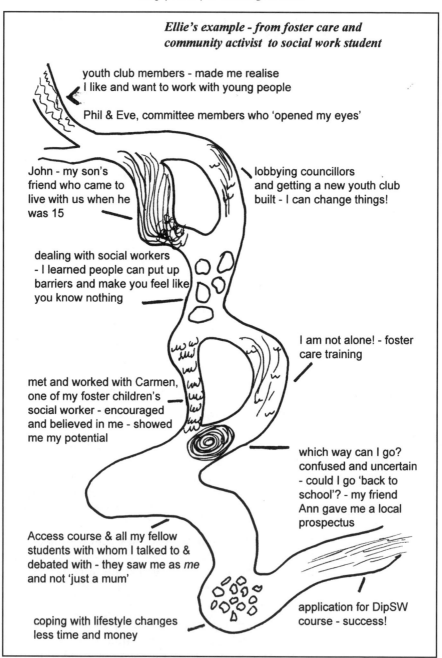

Figure 2. Learning stream.

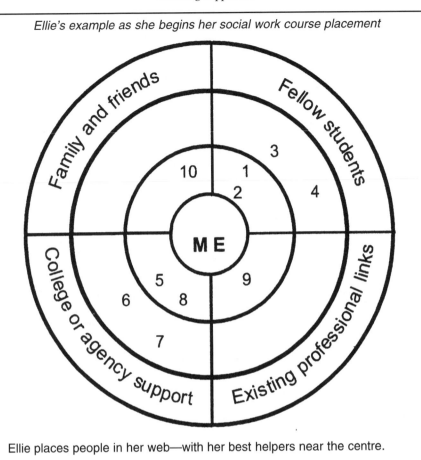

Ellie's example as she begins her social work course placement

Ellie places people in her web—with her best helpers near the centre.

If you can't place people near the centre then maybe you need to look for some extra helpers.

1–3 female colleagues Ellie talks about anything and everything with
  4 John, in her tutorial group who she does not like a lot but who raises lots of points she knows she should be aware of
  5 a lecturer she finds approachable and helpful
  6 her tutor
  7 her practice teacher
  8 member of the team she soon relates to as a role-model
  9 Carmen who remains a mentor
10 her partner who helps her think of other things but work!

Figure 3. Learning web.

There are many ways of visualising relationships between people. For your learning network you need to place people according to their actual or possible helping potential.

Your network is individual to your situation and needs. You need, therefore, to phrase the questions that will provide the appropriate answers for your personal learning context.

Thinking about grouping and identifying learning supporters will be individual, but Figure 4 gives some suggestions.

If your learning needs are focused upon a particular programme or course your questions will probably be very specific to that.

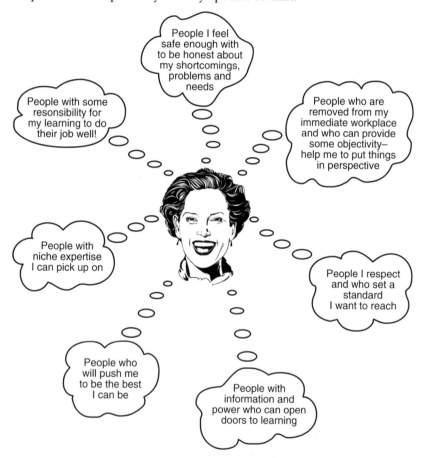

Figure 4. What sort of helpers do I need?

Sometimes it seems preferable to choose people for the comfort factor and not the challenge factor, so try not to take the first or easy option when

> For example, if you are working towards an S/NVQ assessor award you need to ask yourself about the people who can assist you in using the opportunity to learn:
> - who are potential candidates for me to assess?
> - what factors will affect my choice of candidates?
> - do I need to involve anyone else?
> - who will act as an internal verifier for their assessments and mine?
> - who can support me in preparing and making sense of my evidence?
> - are there other people outside the organisation who can help me?

thinking about some of your learning supporters. Conversely, for example, if you are assessing others to provide for your own development needs, and you have a choice of candidates, be aware of the limits of your own resources. Don't overstretch too soon and do the candidate and yourself a disservice.

Summary

This chapter has identified many ways in which other people around you can support your learning. It has also offered you some practical exercises for thinking about the named individuals who can support you in your learning situation. It has also asked you to consider how your learning pathway has been influenced by those around you, either in a helpful or an inhibiting way.

It has also hopefully encouraged you to think about the unique sets of skills and knowledge in those with whom you have contact at work, people that have the potential to assist and inspire you to learn more and learn better.

References

Beresford, P. (1994), *Changing the Culture: Involving Service Users in Social Work Education*, CCETSW Paper 32: 2, London: CCETSW.

CCETSW, (1995 edition), *CCETSW Paper 30*.

CCETSW (1996) *Assuring Quality for Practice Teaching: Rules and Requirements for the Practice Teaching Award: Approval, Review and Inspection of Practice Teaching Programmes*, March 1996, London: CCETSW.

Coles, M. (1998) Top Managers Share Secrets, *The Sunday Times*, 17 May 1998, pp. 7 – 28.

Doel, M., Shardlow, S., Sawdon, C. and Sawdon, D. (1996) *Teaching Social Work Practice*, Aldershot: Arena.

Dwyer, W. (1995) *Staying on the Path*, Carson, C.A.: Hay House Incorporated.

Fowler, A. (1998) Guide Lines, *People Management*, October 15, 1998 pp. 48–50.

Harding, T. and Oldman, H. (1995) *Involving Service Users and Carers in Local Services*, London/Thames Ditton: NISW/Surrey County Council.

Hawkins, P. and Shohet, R. (1989) *Supervision in the Helping Professions*, Milton Keynes: Open University Press.

Hildebrand, J. (1995) Learning through Supervision, A Systemic Approach, in Yelloly M. and Henkel M. (Eds.) (1995) *Learning and Teaching in Social Work*, London: Jessica Kingsley Publishers.

Hope, P. and Pickles, T. (1995) *Performance Appraisal*, Lyme Regis: Russell House Publishing.

Hrafnsdottir, S. (1997) Field Instruction in Social Work Education: A Study of the Views of Field Instructors in Social Work Education at the University of Iceland in *Issues in Social Work Education*, Vol 16: 1 pp. 48–63.

Hunt, J. (1986 2nd edition) *Managing People at Work*, Maidenhead: McGraw-Hill Book Company.

Leigh, A. (1995) *20 Ways to Manage Better*, London: IPM.

Mentor 2000 (1998) What Does A Mentor do, *The Mentor 2000 Reference Manual*, copyright 1991 P. A. Williams, http://home1.gte.net/mntr2000/whatdoes.htm.

MSN (1999) *How to Use Computing Central Chat Rooms*, http://computingcentral.msn.com/help/howtochat.asp.

O'Brien, E. and Hart, S. (1999) Peer learning, *Educational Research*, Vol 41, No 1 Spring 1999, pp. 77–90.

Payne, J. (1999) Defining Lifelong Learning, *Adults Learning*, April 1999 Vol 10 No 8, pp. 9–11.

Pritchard, J. (Ed.) (1995) *Good Practice in Supervision*, London: Jessica Kingsley Publishers.

Raine, A. (1998) Training and Development in Today's Call Centre, *Focus*, November 1998, pp. 16–17.

Ramrayka, L. (1998) Twin Targets, *The Guardian Society*, Wednesday May 20 1998, pp. 8–9.

Reece, B. and Brandt. R. (1996 6th edition) *Effective Human Relations in Organisations*, Boston: Houghton Mifflin Company.

Schwartz, L. (1999) *New Horizon Coaching, Inc.—What's New*, http://www.new-horizon-coaching.com/whatsnew.html.

Shardlow, S. and Doel, M. (1996) *Practice Learning and Teaching*, Basingstoke: Macmillan.

Smale, G. (1996) *Mapping Change and Innovation*, London: HMSO.

Solas, J., (1994) *The (De)Construction of Educational Practice in Social Work*, Aldershot: Avebury.

SSI (1994) *Users' Views on Training for Community Care*, London: DOH.

Swanton, O. and Henshaw, L. (1998) For your own protection, *Guardian Education*, June 23 1998, pp. 2–3.

Taylor, I. (1999) Critical Commentary—Social Work Education, *British Journal of Social Work*, Vol 29 No 1 February 1999, pp. 175–180.

Thompson, A. (1999) High Anxiety, *Community Care*, 1–7 April 1999, pp. 18–19.

Trevillion S. and Beresford, P. (1996), *Meeting the Challenge—Social Work Education and the Community Care Revolution*, London: National Institute for Social Work, London.

Village Project (1997) *Pain and Gain: Village Project Mentors Work to Make a Difference*, http: //courtlink.utcourts.gov/mentors.html, 10/98.

Waldman, J. and Tuson, G. (1997) *Teaching and Learning Development Project Report—Service User Involvement in Basic Social Work Education*, Southampton: University of Southampton.

Waldman, J., Dominelli, L. and Borrill, W. (1997) *Report—Good Practice Teaching in the UK—for CCETSW*, Southampton: University of Southampton.

Yelloly, M. and Henkel, M. (Eds.) (1995) *Learning and Teaching in Social Work*, London: Jessica Kingsley Publishers.

5. Resources for learning

> *Tactics means doing what you can with what you have.*   Saul Alinsky

This chapter is intended to help you take an entrepreneurial approach to finding and using other resources to support your learning needs. Today's expanding market for open learning, aided by technological advancements, puts you in a potentially stronger position to tap in to a wider range of helping materials and resources.

The challenge for the individual may be to create a coherent whole from different sources of learning support. For this reason a section on portfolio building has been included at the end of the chapter. Portfolios are one way of pulling together, in a systematic way, strands of learning that may arise from different sources.

Crucially, the ideas covered in the following pages are intended to encourage you to be more eagle-eyed in observing and using what is going on around you. If you are on a formal work-based learning programme the need to look with fresh eyes at the working environment will probably be intrinsic. If you are learning independently you may need an additional driver to encourage you to stand back in this way.

Not only is the immediate environment a resource for learning but, by reframing what you are experiencing, you may be directed towards other resources that were unnoticed previously. Writing for an audience as an approach to promoting self-directed learning is covered later in the chapter.

Another part of this chapter is devoted to the use of electronically generated or computer-based learning resources and media. Technology has already changed, and is continuing to change, perspectives on teaching and learning in the workplace.

Electronic media has immense potential benefits for the learner. The use of technology needs to begin with an inventory of your needs, followed by an assessment of *how or if* technology can assist.

The answer to the question 'Can a technological solution help you do x or y more quickly or efficiently?' is not always yes, so it is important to fit any assistance to the needs and not vice versa.

Potential resources to support learning are becoming increasingly diverse. Some may impose boundaries and expectations on what is to be learned, but a learner-outlook should encourage you not to be limited by these. Individually there is usually some potential to extend learning programmes to meet other personal learning needs.

Workplace environment

The immediate workplace environment seems an appropriate place to begin to look for resources for learning. These include some of the detail that day-to-day pressures and routines may encourage you to sideline. Adams (1996:324), provides a reminder of what may be missed.

... the big picture is hiding in the details. It's in the clothes, the office supplies, the casual comments and the coffee.

It is important not to become immune to the apparently mundane dimensions of the work environment. Look with fresh eyes at the things that you experience every day.

> I asked a practitioner that I was due to visit, where I should wait when I arrived at her office complex. During the conversation it became clear that she never came in through the front entrance: the initial view of the agency that service users and other visitors experienced was unknown to her. She could not describe the reception area and was unaware of how service users might respond to it on their first visit to the agency. The reception area gives out significant visual messages about the organisation and its attitudes to service users and others.

Two examples of everyday items that can be under-used for learning in the workplace are noticeboards and records.

Noticeboards

Internal noticeboards of various organisations can provide an intriguing insight into these organisations. In community and social work contexts there tend to be noticeboards for staff and those aimed at service users. What information is included, and what by default, gets left off? Are the notices and messages up to date? Are they relevant, eye-catching, easy to understand?

Very often noticeboards can become another picture on the wall. If they hardly change the familiar passer-by just sees them as part of the day-to-day scenery of the workplace and not actually notice the information they contain. Noticing noticeboards is another form of observation in practice.

Events, bulletins, health and safety information, networking ideas can all contribute to a critical engagement with the culture and business of the workplace and help you to stay focused upon the broader context of the organisation and not just your own area of activity or responsibility.

Human beings are often habitual creatures, and many of us have well-worn routine 'visual paths'. Some trainees, when asked to look at the walls of their work setting and later recall this information confirmed how little they had actually taken in of what was on the noticeboards.

Ingham (1997:93) recommends that they should become:

a dynamic space; keep its displays constantly changing so there's something new to stimulate you when you glance in its direction.

Lessons can be learned from the art of window dressing in retail – if it is a paying job then someone is obviously valuing the investment in attracting customers. So what catches your eye on the walls at work?

Records

Management of paperwork or records on databases is one of the challenges facing the contemporary practitioner working with people. For all sorts of reasons, including accountability, records need to be systematically and accurately maintained. Simply staying on top of basic administrative filing, either paper-based or electronic, can be draining and time-consuming. As Welch says:

The tidal wave of the information revolution has hit us hard. (1999:2)

There are no quick fixes to dealing with this task, and further reading ideas are provided at the end of the chapter. It is likely, however, that the paper or e-mail shuffling task is so devoid of stimulation that the learning potential of this information flow may not be fully realised.

Adopting a learning stance to this routine task means using a scanning and storage system that will enable you to filter out the information that can be used for learning, either immediately or in the future.

Example 1

There may be many requests for comments and feedback on memos, meeting agendas or research activities that are downgraded within your 'to do' list of priorities. Reflective learning can be energised, however, by utilising such opportunities for requests in a constructive way.

For example the Open University produces teaching support materials for its associate lecturers. Joe, received a questionnaire asking for feedback on these recently and in one way it presented as a task that would be time-consuming, a little tiresome and yield little direct reward for him. From a learning perspective, however, it provided him with an opportunity to think critically about the materials he had been using regularly and to see how his views on their usefulness had changed and developed. He was given a chance to take another look at whether he was making the most of the materials and what he might do differently. In answering the questions he was provided with an indirect self-assessment tool.

Reflection via filtering

As the last section of this chapter will show, portfolio building is one activity that is helped by an effective filtering system. It involves gathering day-to-day work-generated products that cumulatively builds into a picture that demonstrates evidence of one or more learning criteria. This can often provide a good boost to improving the quality of products you are required to prepare; knowing that they need to serve an additional purpose.

The process of filtering and filing in itself *may* create a significant degree of critical engagement with practice activities. This in turn can provide the fresh perspective mentioned earlier. This involves thinking in a more personalised way about the things that happen day-to-day, from which professional development may arise incrementally.

This is where filed documents can assist in seeing the milestones more clearly. Filing in itself generally only shows levels of competence in a particular administrative skill. But what happens to the files, and how old documents are used is another question. Unless there is a specific requirement to look back, the filing of the documents may be an end in itself.

For the person looking to learn at work, the reading of materials that relate to personal participation can elucidate perceived and actual changes and involvement. Client assessments, reports to committees or managers, programmes produced in a cyclic way, for example in day centres, are all the sort of materials that may give insights. Reading different examples produced over a period of time may be something that does not occur regularly yet it can provide useful indicators of learning progress in a number of areas including skills in:

- assessment
- report writing
- influencing others
- decision-making

The S/NVQ emphasis is on producing materials that show a standard is being met time and time again. Your goal might be to show how you have *raised* the standard time and time again.

Using documentary records that are information-based, if space is available in work schedules, can enhance learning by keeping one updated and engaged. Rather than looking to external information sources it may be surprising how much exists on your doorstep, buried beneath other layers of paperwork.

It is another area where the rationale for encouraging better use of research and best practice dissemination can be understood.

These are limited examples of workplace resources that may offer more scope for assisting personal learning that normal work routines allow for.

There are many others and, of course people, as probably the best resource have been considered in the previous chapter.

Job application forms

Inevitably learning at work will often be concerned with career development. For the student or volunteer this may mean getting through the 'professional door'. For the experienced practitioner this may relate to promotion, a move into management or a new area of specialism.

A useful resource for those who have a goal related to a particular role or area of work is a job application pack, since the materials in these packs can provide a practical and relevant measurement tool for your learning goals.

Most job specifications are now written in a detailed format providing essential and desirable requirements for skills, knowledge, experience and values, in addition to the general expectations of the role and duties of the post. The personal specification is a particularly helpful piece of paper for keeping abreast of current workforce needs. They tell you what employers need *now*. A large company or local authority may well have updated the personnel form for a job specification for any new posts and it might include additional and different requirements, say, possibly more emphasis on IT skills or particular information systems. Applications have to be written to these specifications.

Taking a job specification, perhaps for a post you aspire to, sit down and plot how you would show evidence that you meet the requirements. In doing this, without the pressure of actually applying for the post, you should get a good indication of your current strengths and level of experience.

Filling in application forms now usually means being explicit about how you meet the requirements of the job. It is not enough to write a paragraph on previous experience. You need to be able to extract specific responsibilities and duties and then show how these are relevant to the requirements of the post in question. Being succinct and focused in describing what you actually do every day when you turn up to work is not easy. How can you give full justice to the complexity of your role in a few lines? Such a task may come easier to those educated or trained within such a system.

Writing out a précis of this kind, if done with honesty, is enormously helpful in identifying what you do, rather than talk about generalisations. It will highlight areas that are undeveloped and which require further attention if you aspire to the post in question. It is another means by which you can complete a personal skills audit.

Visits

In the previous chapter the notion of twinning was discussed, which centred on sharing ideas between people in different organisations. Similarly, undertaking constructive visits to other workplace settings can offer considerable insight into practice elsewhere that may offer ideas for improving your own practice. Visits that have a very strict itinerary and supervision are less helpful than those where one can mingle and talk to service users, where appropriate, and staff about their work and the issues they face. Youth work has a strong tradition of valuing the benefits to staff and young people of club visits, inter-club events and Youth Exchange Programmes at a local, regional and national level. If the benefits are understood for young people then it seems reasonable to apply the learning principles to ourselves. Visits can be arranged or you can take advantage of open days, annual general meetings and community events, and use them as opportunities to learn about the work of other agencies.

Community-based sources

Reading materials

Large organisations will be able to provide reading materials and a range of documentary sources from internal libraries. Many people working in smaller organisations, in a single worker role or in a domestic setting may well have to think more laterally with regard to accessing materials as a support to reflecting upon and analysing work-based activities.

Hawtin et al. (1994) identify information or data as hard or soft or quantitative or qualitative. A learner-outlook often means generating for oneself a range of soft data such as the diary material described in Chapter 3. Learners also need, however, help with reframing workplace activities using harder, more objective data.

One of the potential limits of learning at work is that it can be a somewhat introspective activity. If learning includes assessment by colleagues or seniors in the workplace there needs to be confidence that their judgements are informed by a healthy degree of objectivity. Any workplace offers a view of practice but not *the only* view.

Individually you may need to take a proactive approach in seeking out additional learning materials and perspectives. Local libraries should not be underestimated for providing professionally relevant reading. It may not be worth holding out for the most recommended books, better to skim read what is available than nothing at all. Public libraries are also very good in the UK in that specific books can be requested, even if there is sometimes a small charge. Many libraries will have journals and magazines, and for those who feel constrained in their work-based environment the atmosphere of most libraries is conducive to reading without distraction. Even if you cannot take books away you can, as a member of the public, visit university and other educational establishments' libraries and take advantage of their resources.

This includes being able to attend a range of free public lectures, often by well-known professionals in the field.

University bookshops also often have a section for second-hand books and of course many bookshops and jumble sales, particularly in areas around a university will yield good results for reading. Other community organisations such as local councils or community services often have resource libraries and guides on local organisations, either paper-based or on the Internet. Other options are telephone helplines, information and advice services that are aimed at service users primarily.

All the above may seem rather mundane for the experienced person working in a well-resourced organisation but many people in youth and community and social care work still have to battle over the most basic of development resources. Doing work-based programmes such as S/NVQs may not always include college components and thus finding helpful resources may come down to the flexibility and energy of the individual.

Wired up to learn

In the next section the possibilities for technological support are discussed. If access to computer resources is difficult for you, public internet points are possible, again through libraries or in commerical outlets such as cyber cafes.

Moves towards more open learning routes means more possibilities for individual learners to access a wider range of resources to support their learning at work, many technology-based.

It is difficult not to be over enthusiastic when exploring the vast potential of technology for helping people at work to learn. But not everyone may feel as enthusiastic, for a number of reasons. People can take up extreme positions in their stance on technological developments as technophobes or technophiles.

It is likely that to use the benefits of technology without it replacing other foundations of social interaction, a position somewhere in the middle of these two extremes needs to be found. This chapter focuses on information and communications technology for its relevance to learning issues.

In other words the media that has the potential to quicken and diversify access to a range of information sources and ways of exchanging that information with other people. Technological change is still about people and for those of us working in the human services use of technology is not self- serving but should be about improvements to services and service delivery for those we work with.

In thinking about how technology can be a learning resource for you a list of questions is provided in Table 1 to help inform decision-making. Although these questions are aimed at institutions considering their teaching and learning needs, they are adaptable for individual use.

A	Access: how accessible is a particular technology for you? Is it flexible?
C	Costs: what costs would be involved for you or your organisation both for set up and usage?
T	Teaching and learning: what do you want to learn? what sorts of technologies could help any different learning needs you have?
I	Interactivity and user-friendliness: what kinds of interaction does a technology offer and how easy is it to use? Would it involve additional training from others to use it?
O	Organisational issues: are there barriers in your organisation that would prevent the use of this technology, including cultural ones?
N	New: is the technology tried and tested? If use involves other people will they have it too?
S	Speed: how long would it take to begin using it?

(Adapted from Bates, 1995:1)

Table 1. Can technology help me and how?

These questions are a useful reminder of the stance individual learners need to take to technology. Technology cannot be seen as some kind of catch all solution to learning problems. Viewing and using technology must be done as critically as for any other form of training and learning. Web-based material is largely uncensored so you need to ask about its validity and reliability.

It should be used to enhance and enable particular learning needs. Technological solutions must be considered alongside other methods and supportive resources for teaching and learning. As Bates (1995:13) says:

There is no 'super-technology'—all technologies have their strengths and weaknesses.

So in essence what can technology do to help you meet your learning needs and which ones can deliver what you want?

Learning technologies encompass a wide range of applications and systems.

They can range from use of a tape recorder, to the use of a word processor, to computer-based interactive learning courses, in which all communication between a learner and the course provider is done via electronic communication.

Bates (1995) identifies that in essence there are two distinctions in the technology: primarily one-way or two-way communication. He alerts us to the eroding distinctions between media and technologies as the capabilities of single machines grow.

In part the interactive scope has been described in the previous chapter. Not surprisingly technology for education and training has been advanced by the practical needs arising from distance-based teaching and learning in countries such as Canada and Australia.

Increasingly technology can assist in enhancing the potential for work-based learning by bringing more of the learning activities associated with the classroom to the learner, wherever they may be.

Even more traditional access to learning resoures such as television is in transition. Whilst at the moment use of television is largely one way via programme broadcasting, digital television means the development of more interactive uses for this medium. Currently there is a wealth of free educational material on the radio or television that can be used by the isolated work-based learner – in the UK notably Open University programming. In the future there will much more use of commercially-based educational programming which the customer chooses to buy into, as with existing satellite and cable channels. There exists now a degree of interactivity with telephone phone-in links.

There is a wide difference in access to some of the various forms of technology-based resources. For example, some organisations will choose to operate their own electronic mail system, an intra-net system, and may restrict the use of Internet access for financial and human resource reasons. Others may still be without computers at all. Indeed, there is still much work to be done on knowing how to enable workers to learn from rather than be alienated by the information Superhighway and technological learning tools (Gray,1999).

The practice example below shows, however, many of the possibilities for technology in providing a gateway to learning resources that may be based either in the next room or on the other side of the globe.

It is intended to:

- encourage you to consider the range of options for using technology to support your learning
- remind you of the more traditional options, such as doing an audio or video tape of a piece of practice
- help you act locally and think globally with the information resource that is the Internet

---

A practice example of problem-solving using technology.

Background
Dan is seconded to develop a new initiative within a residential unit for learning disabled young adults; to provide a short term respite and treatment programme for people with severe challenging behaviour in a refurbished wing.

Supportive context

He was encouraged by his manager to address the learning elements for the new initiative which would highlight him personally amongst the staff team. On the agenda for each weekly team meeting was an item called 'learning points' where staff members were encouraged to raise questions and to bring individual ideas for collective resolution.

The issues and problem

Dan realised he had a steep learning curve ahead of him because although he had lots of experience of the service user group and in residential settings, the particular focus of the initiative was new to him.

He prioritised two aspects of his learning as follows:

- to find examples of good practice from elsewhere
- to plan monitoring and evaluation activities for the new initiative

Limitations and opportunities for accessing learning support

Due to the shift work pattern of his hours, Dan found he had difficulty in accessing his local library, and the one at the head office of his organisation, for reading materials and library searches. Similarly, he also found it difficult ringing people during work hours.

He did identify some quiet periods on two of the shifts when he could devote some time to do some information gathering.

The unit had a computer with a modem for use by staff and residents with supervision. To date he had not used this resource very much.

The plan

Dan felt that by using the computer to find out the information he wanted he would not only meet his need for finding good practice examples, but also improve his skills and confidence with using the Internet as he had a purpose for 'playing about' with it.

He asked one of the residents who liked using the Internet for help with using the search engines; deciding which ones were the best and refining the search tools.

Outcomes for Dan and the initiative

He found world wide web sites with information on, and printed off key pages about the sorts of issues he was facing in his work.

⇩

Two projects he thought sounded very interesting; one based in Ohio and one based in Cardiff.

⇩

He e-mailed the contact listed for the Ohio project and phoned the Cardiff person with the following outcomes:

- From the Ohio link he exchanged ideas and generated an opportunity for an electronic pen-pal scheme between the residents in the two units. He was also given ideas on where to look up research reports on the world wide web.

⇩

- He received an invite to Cardiff to visit the project there and was also shown an example of a cd rom research module that covered evaluation methods.

⇩

- He persuaded his manager to ask the training manager to purchase the cd rom learning programme for the organisation as a whole.

⇩

- He significantly improved his skills in using and understanding of the Internet.

Writing

No matter how good our intentions are to make space in the day to bring into focus our learning goals, sometimes an additional motivator or structured guidance is required to keep us going . Many of the resources in this chapter and in Chapter 6 can provide this kick-start. It is, however, not merely as padding that study guides usually include a section on the student who procrastinates, with tips such as '10 ways of delaying starting on homework'.

Learning at work is no different; in fact the perfect excuses for not starting or completing learning related tasks surround you all day long. It is easy to present an effective argument for prioritising 'real' work and 'very important' tasks. At some point, however, it may have to be acknowledged that the appointments diary is being used as an avoidance strategy.

For some who know that they need the extra push to get on with the business of learning at work this can be provided by an external educational programme that includes practice-focused assignments.

For many people, however, attendance on such a programme is not an option for all sorts of reasons, not least financial or personal, i.e. if caring for a housebound person.

Writing with intent can provide an alternative activity for those who need to see a product or outcome of their reflections and 'internal research'.

Writing is valuable for stepping back and exploring in a systematic way issues that arise in the workplace for which there is no outlet within supervision or the formal record keeping processes. Writing can channel thoughts and feelings that can sometimes fester and turn into frustrations as they constantly simmer away in the background.

Keiller (1989:139) describes the process of writing as:

a means of discovery, always when you come to the end . . . you'll know something you didn't when you began.

That something may turn out to be not be much at all. On the other hand it could turn out to be a rewarding experience for you that may also benefit others.

No doubt many people dream of one day turning their life experiences into a great novel. Not all of course, turn dream into a reality. Do you recall the SMART objectives in Chapter 3? Apply them to a writing goal that involves action and a positive outcome is much more likely.

Even playing SMART may be easier said than done. Where do you start? What do you write about? The logical sequence of thinking, planning and action applies here as with other activities. Take time just to think yourself in to the idea of sitting down and writing, of putting pen to paper or finger to keyboard. Yeger (1994:6) sums up feelings that she sees in the process of beginning.

You, dreaming of being a writer, know instinctively that once you begin the journey there will be no turning back. Pandora's box will spring open, and everything will be terrible and wonderful, life enhancing, overwhelming and totally revolutionary. Your journey will lead you away from the safe, the predictable, the structured, the organised, into a landscape which is both utterly familiar and terrifyingly strange. Powerful and painful.

Is it any wonder that you sharpen pencils, tidy drawers, clean, cook, sew, use any excuse rather than pick up the pen and write? But . . . admitting the fear and trying to analyse what lies behind it could be the first step on the journey.

Yeger's evocative words allow us to imagine both the possibilities of writing and also the reality of getting down to it, feelings that may echo with taking control of your own learning in general. Of course this kind of felt response may not arise at all and you may be able to go straight from idea to action. For many people they may first need to think and may ask.

What have I got to say that's worth saying at all?

If you work with people in interesting or challenging situations you probably have quite a lot to say.

Do you start with an audience in mind or just get going?

A bit of both. If writing is new to you a first stage might just be to practise holding an idea and putting it down on paper or on a tape recorder, allowing it to grow and expand at will. Speaking your thoughts is no different to writing them. Capturing fleeting thoughts and ideas on a dictaphone can be as easy as jotting them down on paper or a personal organiser or electronic notebook and no less valid. Do not worry about form or structure when you begin. Enjoy the mental freedom of letting your thoughts wander where they want to go, unfettered by somebody's else's agenda.

At some point you will feel ready to either continue with your personal writing or perhaps progress to writing for an audience.

Preparation is key

Don't aim to start with the doorstopper, start with a 300–400 word article for an in-house or organisational newsletter or a letter to a newspaper about an issue you feel strongly about.

Whatever you decide to start with, narrow the field down and make a decision about the particular type of publication and audience you want to aim for. If you wish to produce an article for a magazine, a world wide web journal, or a letter to a newspaper, then do your background work first. Be clear about the submission requirements for the newsletter, feature page or journal. Consider:

- length
- presentation
- format for submission
- thematic issues?
- style
- time-scales for consideration and submission of articles
- feedback

Whether you are accepted or not, the feedback you get on your writing, especially for academic journals, can provide a huge learning opportunity. The process of researching outlets for writing can also provide a domino effect for your development, in that through researching journals for style, content and how to submit articles, you will also be reading up to date material and thus doing two learning activities at once. There is no point in writing a fantastic article if someone else addressed much the same topic in the previous edition. It is a humbling experience to realise there is no such thing as original thought!

If your work is accepted there is then the additional phase of facing up to the public scrutiny of your thoughts, ideas and perhaps things you feel very strongly about which other people then challenge. Venturing out in to the world of public speaking and writing can certainly be one of the areas of risk-taking discussed in Chapter 2.

Co-writing

One of the ways of dissipating some of the potential isolation of working alone and extending peer learning opportunities is by joint writing. This is certainly not necessarily an easier option; it can test negotiating and feedback skills fully when constructing pieces of writing as a pair or group endeavour. Writing collaboratively can be a fascinating and stimulating experience, and there is much satisfaction to be gained from working with, say, students and young people (see Waldman, Glover and King, 1999, Waldman and Hague, 1996).

The process provides a different way of engaging with colleagues and others and can lead to new levels of insight into experience and understandings. For those needing additional support and motivation writing as part of a group clearly provides additional help and structure.

If possibilities are not available from those in your existing personal or professional networks then seeking out other collaborators may be worthwhile, perhaps by joining an adult education writing group. It is still possible to use this as a route to writing about professional interests.

Confidentiality issues have to be addressed in whatever writing context you choose. Sharing thoughts and ideas with those who do not have the intimate reference points of the practice clique requires an explicitness and transparency in the articulation of those ideas that can only help to sharpen analytical and writing skills.

Who can write?

The creation of professional knowledge continues to be contested, with an ongoing tussle for status between 'academic' and 'practice' knowledge. The wider the range of writers entering the public arena the greater the chance there is for the views of many groups silenced within traditional arenas of theory making to be heard and included. Butler and Wintram (1991), describe their understanding of the experience of writing as social work practitioners, about their feminist group-work.

> *The deconstruction of the word writer acts as a release from the constraints of language and artistic ability, where, rather than being seen as a gift, writing becomes a skill which can be learnt. For ourselves as women who sometimes write, collectivity is also mirrored in our methods of writing, where 'we', rather than 'I' or 'she' becomes a conscious statement about women writing together, as well as women being together in groups.* (1991:22)

They cite Itzin's words (1987:115) as a reminder of the possibilities for writing to invoke change at both a personal and public level.

> *As our writing is our thinking, it is a powerful tool in our own and everyone's liberation.*

Whilst the emancipatory potential of writing may seem beyond the modest scope of many, a number of practitioners embarking on new initiatives are often helped the most by examples of other similar practice initiatives and the experiences of others. As the practice example showed, this is where the world wide web can come in its own. Publication in journals or professional arenas may seem too much hassle for some, but anyone can publicise on the Internet, via a personal web site or newsgroup or bulletin boards for example. As the previous section indicated, however, when reading, treat with caution, as lack of censorship and editorial standards bring the need for a highly critical and careful use of materials.

Personal resources and portfolios

The last section of this chapter is devoted to the use of portfolios for managing individual learning records.

Portfolio assessment is not new. Students on art courses, for example have been part of portfolio-based assessments involving the creation of physical products for decades.

Life storybooks used in reminiscence and identity work are a form of portfolio. They serve a very personal function for children or others who need an external resource to assist them in understanding their present through what happened in their past.

A learning portfolio may be defined as point of capture for different pieces of evidence that, when brought together, demonstrate an individual's achievements, activities, efforts and abilities in relation to a specified area or areas of work.

This collection of items may be physical, such as activities designed for and done with children by playworkers.

A more common presentation of portfolios associated with work-based learning is in a folder or set of folders or box file.

Portfolios may now be stored on a single disk or cd rom with the disk files acting as an alternative for paper-based storage systems. These portfolios might contain images and documents downloaded from:

- word processing programmes
- the world wide web
- e-mails
- attachments sent via electronic communication
- scanned pictures, diagrams or photos

Portfolios may be:

Illustrative—containing samples of what someone has produced within their learning-related activities.

Comprehensive—containing all that someone has produced related to the learning purpose of that particular portfolio.

(Adapted from Moran J, 1997:112)

Many of us will assemble portfolios of work-related activities for our own career purposes or just for reminiscence. Figure 2 is illustrative of the type of artefacts such a portfolio might contain.

Purpose

Portfolios can serve a variety of purposes but in relation to learning they are usually linked to self-assessment activities, even at a simple level.

Portfolio building might be linked to very tightly defined guidelines, or it might be entirely designed and assembled to the specifications and needs of the learner.

Portfolios whether simple or complex, will have certain characteristics and involve:

Formative assessment: to enable assessment of different stages in your learning progress.

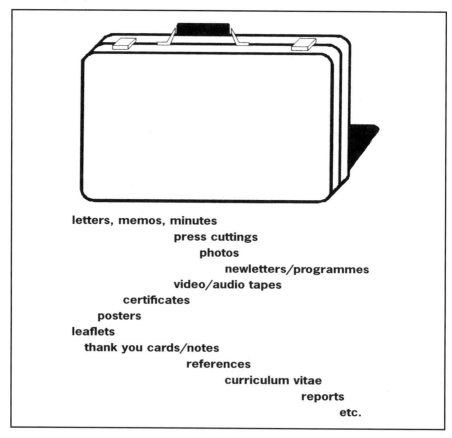

Figure 2. Portfolio contents.

Summative assessment: involving a judgement about the sum of the learning, generally for the purposes of a qualification or award, and therefore to be seen by other people.

The audience for the portfolio is likely to affect significantly the type of material that it contains. It is not uncommon for formative self-assessments to include material for personal use that is not then included in the portfolio for public consumption.

Careful consideration of storage issues in relation to material of a sensitive or confidential nature is a must, whatever the type of portfolio you produce. Deleting any references that could potentially identify someone is of particular importance if you include materials such as case studies, any type of records that refer to individual clients or service users.

Your organisation may have strict guidelines about copying and using client or service user data, so it is vital that you are proactive in familiarising yourself with protocols or policies. You may even need to consider getting a manager or senior member of the organisation to countersign some materials.

It is likely that any learning portfolio will help with some or all of the following:

reflecting	It is a focus for reflective practice activities.
remembering	The contents will help with remembering the chronology of events, the situations themselves and how you felt at the time.
reminding	A portfolio is real and its presence nudges you to stay an active learner.
recording	It offers a way of bringing together in a systematic way information of specific relevance to your learning and development.
reframing	From the range of items you can be helped to put pieces of your learning progress together, perhaps in new ways to aid new perspectives.
recurring	Using portfolios is as much about an approach to continuous learning as it is about the product itself.
representing	As a product it is an ambassador for your own learning.

Contents

It is hard to generalise about portfolio contents because these will depend upon why you are putting the portfolio together in the first place, but whatever is in, there are some general planning issues that are worth considering before you begin.

The key to successful portfolios is the ease with which the reader can navigate its contents. Very often portfolios are a collection of diverse materials that in style or presentation have no uniformity. It is easy for these to present as a messy jumble of papers and other bits and bobs. Even if you as the creator are the only one reading it, a portfolio is like any other personal filing system – there has to be a logic and order about it.

The availability of simple but labour saving devices such as plastic wallets is a straightforward help for the portfolio builder. You will have to weigh up, however, whether you feel the environmental cost overrides the time saving benefits!

If you are assembling a paper-based portfolio in a file, plastic wallets allow you to add and take away material, moving it around with ease, something that happens often with evolving portfolios.

A focus on simple referencing and navigation should be to the forefront of your mind whatever the storage system you adopt.

The importance of concise introductions

The first part of the portfolio should contain a clear guide for the reader. It should convey:

- the purpose of the portfolio
- the range of contents
- any guidance for the reader you feel is necessary on how they should be reading or using the portfolio

In many situations where you are producing a portfolio for a course or an S/NVQ award, for example, you will have to include information to meet regulations and requirements. This may include registration proformas and often biographical details.

Indexing

Having considered the navigation issues a numbered index at the beginning will normally correspond to the relevant items in the portfolio.

Very often one item may relate to several learning criteria so the search for the simplest approach to cross-referencing is advisable.

A basic numbering system is effective within a large portfolio requiring extensive cross-referencing. An item always keeps the same number to avoid confusion. You may divide your evidence into different sections under different headings representing the various learning activities you have been involved in, such as learning logs.

Being selective about what to include

Portfolio building often engenders magpie-like instincts, and anything that might possibly be of use is copied and retained. In the early stages this approach is probably useful, to develop the habits of retrieval and storage.

If you are very organised and focused you may be able to match up an item to a specific learning goal or criteria as you go along. As many of us are not that focused, you may find a collection box useful; a place where you hold materials for sorting later, when you will also decide what items to include and what to discard.

A good self-editor will try not to be too precious about items that may have some personal significance but are not relevant for the portfolio. When building work-based portfolios it is likely you will be able to generate a forest's worth of materials, so the two stage filing can again be helpful.

Declaring the targets and the way markers

The purpose of portfolios is often guided by a set of externally defined requirements and this will include guidance for assembling the portfolio. It is also true that portfolios are individual and that the learner has different degrees of discretion about the end product. This discretion may encompass defining personal learning needs and setting goals associated with those needs, activities described in Chapter 3. These are then likely to form part of the early part of the portfolio, providing a context to the material.

Work-based portfolios in the UK are commonly designed around evidencing competences, as with S/NVQs, or demonstrating learning outcomes. In either of these situations the learning criteria are likely to be very specific.

All material that goes in to the portfolio must, therefore, be shown to have an unambiguous and clearly stated connection to one or more of these criteria. No material should be included as padding or because it represents a work success you are especially proud of.

Unless you have signposted its usefulness in helping to show you have met the learning criteria leave it out.

Combining different sorts of items

Many portfolios linked to work-based learning will be the place to collate the records of the reflective practice activities you are encouraged to undertake. Again these may be the learning diaries or logs, sheets, jottings, mind maps etc., discussed in Chapter 3.

These will often be very personal and again you may want to use a process of selection to include sections or edited versions of material in any portfolios that have a wider audience. The other products or pieces of evidence you put in such as letters, memos, testimonials from colleagues, photos, pictures etc. may stand alone in relation to learning criteria or be linked to other reflective activities.

The choice about whether different materials are clustered together around particular criteria or placed in sections according to the types of evidence will be a decision you will need to make, hopefully with the support of someone else at your workplace.

Time

It is hard to quantify the time needed to complete portfolios. The ease with which you assemble one will depend upon a number of things, not least whether you have used the particular combination of administrative and thinking skills in other circumstances. Portfolio building can be very demanding, but it has a number of benefits for the individual learning at work, whether they do it as part of a course or development programme, or as a result of personal initiative.

Building your own work-based learning portfolio may:

- Help to develop and sustain your learner-outlook.
- Be a reference tool in applying for jobs or courses and relating portfolio evidence to person specifications.
- Assist in self-ssessment by addressing current skills strengths and hopefully development needs.
- Be used for the accreditation of prior achievement and learning – for entry on to courses or to gain credits for work done.
- Enable piecemeal continuing professional development activities to form a coherent whole that can be used for professional and or academic accreditation.

References

Adams, S. (1996) *The Dilbert Principle*, London: Boxtree Ltd.

Alinsky, S. (1971) *Rules for Radicals*, New York:Vintage Books.

Bates, A. (1995) *Technology, Open Learning and Distance Learning*, London: Routledge Studies in Distance Education.

Butler, S. and Wintram, C. (1991) *Feminist Groupwork*, London: Sage Publications.

Cooper, D. (1998) *The VQ Centre Pathways Guide, K201 Working with Young People*, Milton Keynes: The Open University.

Gray, (1999) The Internet in Lifelong Learning: Liberation or Alienation?, *International Journal of Lifelong Education*, Vol 18 No. 2 March–April 1999, pp. 119–126.

Hawtin, M. Hughes, G. and Percy-Smith, J. (1994) *Community Profiling, Auditing Social Needs*, Buckingham: Open University Press.

Hopkins, G. (1998) *The Write Stuff—A Guide to Effective Writing in Social Care and Related Services*, Lyme Regis: Russell House Publishing.

Hopkins, G. (1998) *Plain English for Social Services*, Lyme Regis: Russell House Publishing.

Ingham, C. (1997) *101 Ways to Motivate Yourself*, London: Kogan Page.

Itzin, C. (1987) Head, Hand, Heart—And the Writing of Wrongs, in Sanders, L. (Ed.) *Glancing Fires: an Investigation into Women's Creativity*, London: Women's Press.

Keiller, G. (1989) *We are Still Married*, London: Faber and Faber.

Magee, P. (1999) *Brain Dancing: Work Smarter, Learn Faster and Manage Information More*, Hara Publishing.

Moran, J. (1997) *Assessing Adult Learning*, Kreiger Publishing Company: Malabar, Florida.

Sanders, L. (Ed.) *Glancing Fires: An Investigation into Women's Creativity*, London: Women's Press.

Sellars, S. (Ed.) (1994 2nd edition) *Taking Reality by Surprise—Writing for Pleasure and Publication*, London: The Women's Press.

Vickers, A. (1992) *A Portfolio Approach to Personal and Career Development—Resource Book*, Milton Keynes: The Open University.

Waldman, J., Glover, N. and King, L. (1999) Readiness to Learn—An Experiential Perspective, *Social Work Education*, 18:2. 219 – 228.

Waldman, J. and Hague, F. (1996) Modelling Mutuality: Doing Research with, not on Young People, *Young People Now*, Issue 89 September 1996 pp. 28–29.

Welch, J. (1999) How to . . . Cut Down Your Hours, *The Guardian*, May 1 1999, pp. 2.

Yeger, S. (1994) I've Always Wanted to Write But, in Sellars, S. (Ed.) *Taking Reality by Surprise—Writing for Pleasure and Publication*, London: The Women's Press.

6. Research for learning

> *Research conducted by practitioners is an idea whose time has come.*
> Roger Fuller and Alison Petch (1995:3)

This chapter is concerned, explicitly, with the potential for learning by using the workplace as a research environment, extending the learner-outlook to encompass a role as researcher.

The stance of researcher offers an alternative framework for action that can provide guidance for good practice. This framework is an encouragement to:

- Maintain an open and enquiring mind.
- Be curious and questioning about the events, people and issues that surround you.
- Look for ways in which systems and processes can be improved.
- Value the need for quality information and methods of collecting such information.
- Approach tasks and problem-solving in a systematic way.
- Recognise the limitations and possibilities in personal roles and responsibilities.
- Provide a bridge between personal and collective change.

Why use research to learn?

Identifying with the role of learner as researcher, or vice versa, offers potential for sharpening the critical edge in your practice and possibly that of others around you.

In part a research perspective can provide a means of framing and understanding organisational issues and change initiatives. Zuber-Skeritt (1996:83), identifies broader opportunities within the role of action researcher:

> *. . . emancipatory action research is organisational change 'best practice' . . . it fosters organisational learning and the development of the 'learning organisation'.*

A key word here is emancipatory. Research does not merely take a technicist approach but is 'a collaborative, critical and self-critical inquiry by practitioners' (Zuber-Skeritt, 1996:84). It thus encompasses an underpinning ethical and value position for the role of researcher.

Whilst a learner-outlook can justifiably be 'selfish' in that the primary beneficiary of the learning will be the learner, it also needs to carry out the learning in ways that are consistent with values of human service professionals. One of these infers participation rather than objectification of those people involved in the research/learning.

Stringer (1996) asserts that, whilst there are different definitions of action research, the notion of the subject as active participant is a central thread between them, and names this a 'moral intertwining' of all participants including the researcher. Later on in this chapter the implications of this intertwining will be discussed in more detail.

Atkins (1984), more than a decade ago, argued that:

> *the increasingly sophisticated use of in-service training has highlighted the possibilities of small scale research as part of the facilitation of heightened professionalism in many areas.*

Action research, in being focused upon the work setting, can help to overcome the problem of application of policies, theories and research findings designed for a universal response to issues. These may fail to penetrate the lived reality of day-to-day work experiences.

The struggle for enabling practitioners to refine their own solutions to overcoming *their* problems may be helped through personal research projects. This should emphasise *qualitative* approaches to action research because this should encourage the practitioner researcher to incorporate a self-reflexive, and thus explicit learning dimension to their work.

Within a health and social care context research in practice has gained credence with the developing concept of evidence-based practice. This suggests that practice developments should be grounded in proof of the things that work and this in turn points to some form of research to provide the evidence. For example, the University of Exeter's Centre for Evidence-based Social Services has been funded by the Department of Health to examine policy and practice in research evidence. Aims of the centre are to:

- Translate the results of existing research into service and practice development.
- Ensure research findings are available to Social Services Departments when reviewing and changing service delivery.
- Improve dissemination of relevant research findings (Ashton, 1998:8).

Functional research skills

As many employers and agencies will be able to access only limited numbers of research grants there is increasing attention being given to other ways of developing, disseminating and utilising research work. It is now viewed as acceptable and indeed good practice to promote a research culture within the organisation, whereby practitioners become competent at *using* research evidence as well as generating it themselves.

It may be that your own skills audit, detailed in Chapter 3, has revealed a need for extra help to bump start your confidence in carrying out research, confidence because it is likely that you will have skills that are transferable into a research context such as:

- listening skills
- assessment skills
- time-management skills
- recording and report writing skills
- project management skills

The workplace offers a rich source of research possibilities. It is often a small thing that will generate a nagging curiosity, or a previously unseen connection that triggers a desire for deeper understanding.

Research is not owned by professional researchers. The skills and styles of a researcher can be acquired, adapted and used by volunteers, paid practitioners and others to meet their own needs. Many service users and carers become very skilled researchers as a result of their need to know more about their situation or condition.

Research implies an unresolved question and a plan for how to find that answer. In a work culture increasingly focused on outcome-driven perfomances and activities the end product is often predetermined. A research question can provide a refreshing alternative to this framework. It allows the ending to remain uncertain.

A key aspect of the stance of researcher is, therefore, to be able to stand back and generate the questions:
Why? How? What if?

Friedman (1998) describes research as a passion because 'researchers are truly driven to obtain the answers to their questions'.

It will not, however, always be expedient to ask difficult questions at work. This may be due to:

- internal politics
- workload
- demands of other monitoring and review activities
- the emotional investment needed

The above represent just a few of the barriers that can be put up to inhibit an internally focused enquiry.

In contrast, however, an activity framed as research can also offer a way round some of these barriers. It can make the unknown and the uncertain acceptable.

Practice example:

> A manager within a private foster care agency identified a trend in the recruitment and retention of foster carers looking after teenagers. It indicated a higher drop-out of these carers than with carers looking after other groups. Rather than focusing on the individual members of staff and carers, the manager realised the problem might more helpfully be addressed by objectifying the issue as a question to be tackled within a research project. This deflected a naming and blaming situation with individual carers and members of staff.

Ideas for undertaking research in the workplace

The remainder of this chapter will examine the ways in which opportunities for research in the workplace present themselves. The focus will be upon action research as this is generally concerned with some form of internal enquiry in which the practitioner has an inside relationship with the research question and research subjects. Attention will also be given to methodological approaches that are likely to be accessible for the action researcher.

An outline of a small scale work-based research project will then be used to illustrate the possibilities for and processes involved in research at work . In a single chapter it is not possible to cover in detail how to conduct your research project but the reading list at the end provides suggestions for other helpful material.

The practitioner as action researcher

Bell (1987) argues for action research as a term of many definitions but, in relation to the purpose of this book, she points out that:

> . . . *an important feature of action research is that the task is not finished when the project ends. The participants continue to review, evaluate and improve practice.*

In other words the research process forms not only a problem-solving mechanism but also promotes learning as an intrinsic part of the research activity.

There are a number of strengths and limitations inherent in taking an action research approach. It is important to explore these in relation to your own work setting and personal situation. They may also help you think of other problems or advantages of having an 'inside' position.

The inside position itself can be perceived as *the* problem of action research (National Extension College, 1992). It is the contextual issues that may be associated with this inside position that need to be unpicked and made explicit. Each individual needs to explore whether these present as disadvantages or advantages for the piece of work they wish to do.

Research, in a sense, gives you permission to stand back and ask sometimes difficult questions of events and people around you at work.

The objectification of a problem as an *interesting issue*, rather than focusing on failure, may help to mitigate against potential defensiveness amongst peers. The practitioner researcher must negotiate a fine balance in their role as colleague and researcher.

The impact of an inside position cannot be negated. It is important to think through the issues and possible consequences of this shift in role, especially if the research involves questioning work colleagues. It is naive to assume that history can be set aside whilst the research is being conducted and there may be gains or losses in relationships by undertaking the research. What happens if people do not like what your research reveals?

Researcher as learner

Returning to the notion of researcher as learner, this role can provide a 'curriculum' to learning activities through the framework of:

- principles
- objectives
- tasks

The answers to the question you choose to address may actually be secondary to the insights you gain trying to find them.

This is not, however, a recommendation to ask people to give time and assistance merely to a 'paper exercise'. Rather, in many circumstances it may be prudent to be modest in the aspirations regarding the influence of your research. Full time researchers have to cope with this kind of realism too. Take, for example the introductory dedication Robinson (1993) often uses in presentations:

> . . . to all those educational researchers who have wished that educational practitioners and policy-makers would take more notice of their work.

Sometimes it is hard to accept that your own enthusiasm for your work and findings is not shared equally by others!

Approaches to work based research

From the stance of researcher-learner, there are two qualitative research approaches which are of particular relevance to work-based research.

These represent a small range, but for many practitioners they may provide an accessible way in to conducting primary research alongside work commitments. Which is not to suggest that other approaches should or cannot be used, including quantitative methods.

Possible pitfalls in internal research

It is unfortunate that many people who are not 'professional' researchers often associate research with questionnaires. They may too quickly look to use quantitative methods such as surveys, as if credibility is necessarily bound up by the presence of statistics.

The reality of practitioner research situations is that activities such as surveys may involve imposing an ill-fitting approach to a research question. I use the example of a report completed by a practitioner which had taken a survey-based approach and which contained wonderful graphical images of statistics. The focus on the glossy presentation wrapped up a content was derived from closed questions with 20 people and dressed up as representing the views of a community.

Use of quantitative data may emerge more naturally from documentary analysis of records and statistics that are kept as a part of normal procedures. Some organisations wishing to do research know that they have a wealth of useful data within existing records but did not have the time to collate and analyse it themselves.

If action research can help you to utilise existing material for a wider range of purposes then that seems a positive learning outcome for you and, hopefully, your organisation. Chapter 7 addresses ways of accessing and utilising routinely gathered data.

A small scale approach does not mean a piece of work cannot generate valid and useful data, the danger is in the researcher being seduced by the false assumption that research = big + all + large numbers:

As Bell (1987:102) says:

> *in a 100 hour project generalisation is unlikely, but relatability may be entirely possible.*

Go for quality, not necessarily quantity. For the action researcher the expectation is that the research outcomes will have applicability in a very tangible and localised way. Generalisation is rarely the goal so why try to build this in when you have no need of it and cannot achieve it? The key is quality, whatever the size of the project, to be able to show:

> *. . . practitioner action research as an activity that represents both a powerful, vigorous and worthwhile form of practical professionalism and a powerful, vigorous and valid form of social enquiry.* (Winter, 1996:25)

A key word here is professionalism. The researcher-practitioner has to maintain a conscious reflexivity about the research work in which they are engaged and its relationship to the activities of others in the workplace. As Winter (1996:23) says:

> *We note not only the contradictions in others' viewpoints, but also the contradictions and possibilities for change in our own viewpoints. We are not*

consultants, advising others how to change . . . We are part of the situation undergoing change. We have no theoretical basis for exempting ourselves from the processes we set in motion.*

The researcher may act as a catalyst for change and this is just as likely to arise from the process of doing the research as the results it generates. Alasuutari's (1995) uses the rather apt notion of 'unriddling' to describe the process of interpreting or reframing our understandings of phenomena and data.

How the researcher-learner role can help you learn

A learner who is both a practitioner and a researcher may find they are engaged in a process of enquiry that assists them in sense-making of their experiences with a specific set of tools, in this context research tools. They may be able to share this sense-making in an empowering way with others around them.

Everyone should find a set of tools that is appropriate to their own research question or objectives, but which also integrate well with existing working practices and activities.

The frames below summarise some of the ways in which action research can help you to learn and also the things that you may need to sidestep or deal with for it to be effective.

- Allows you to stand back and take up a position of critical distance.
- Provides a route to asking potentially challenging questions of your work environment.
- Provides a medium for critique and reflection.
- Provides a purpose and framework for your learning and even a curriculum.
- Makes you think hard about professional values concerned with concepts such as 'partnership', 'empowerment' and 'participation'; how you 'do' these things rather than just espouse them.
- Motivates you because what you do might influence positive change in your practice and those of people around you.
- Helps you refine skills in such areas as communication and project management.
- Helps you to engage differently with your existing knowledge.

Potential issues that may need to be tackled from the inside position include:

- Establishing what the questions 'for whom' and 'by whom' mean in your piece of research.
- Research activity can distract you from your 'real' work so focus upon your project and time-management skills.
- Make sure you are able to follow through your research plan. You have made a commitment to others, not just yourself.

You may be at a different stage to others around you with the research question because you have been focusing upon it intensely – don't expect others to be at the same place as you! You may say or do the same thing, but to different people and therefore be perceived as inspiring or boring or threatening, depending upon the other person's position and viewpoint.

- Be prepared for a position of risk, where your views and conclusions will be challenged by people who are also very familiar with the issues you are researching.
- Be prepared for the consequences of what your research might reveal, for you personally, others you work with (including colleagues and service users) and the organisation. Your findings might say things that people do not want to hear and you will be around for the messy phase of deciding how to respond to them. Outside researchers are often only obliged to do the research and then leave the agency to sort out solutions for themselves. Can you maintain a critical distance when faced with criticism of your own work, feedback that might also be a catalyst for your learning?
- You need to be constantly checking out what you are doing to ensure you are not making assumptions or being biased because you are familiar with the setting. This constant reflexivity can be difficult to sustain.

The following two approaches, which will be examined in more detail, may also be perceived as a development of some of the reflective learning activities discussed in Chapter 3. The approaches may involve utilising different methods of data collection including:

- interviews with semi-structured questions
- interviews with an open narrative more in the tradition of oral history
- participant observation
- diaries
- descriptive recording
- checklists
- analysis of documentary data

A cautionary note

There are various methods of data collection and the reading list at the end of the chapter offers various starting points that can help you select the ones that best suit your research needs.

The emphasis on the two approaches below is to help you to think carefully about the nature of research as it relates to your learning in the workplace. They will assist you to question and engage with the possibilities and consequences of research rather than providing a description of research techniques which are already amply provided in existing literature and computer-based resources.

Bell (1987) describes action research as a separate approach to the ones described below, but they can be appropriately used within an action research model. Methods, approaches, models and styles are terms that are sometimes used interchangeably, and here action-research is presented as a stance which can adopt either of the approaches below.

- case study analysis
- problem based approaches

Case study analysis

Case study analysis seems a useful way to build a research perspective into your work. Stake (1995) argues that it is difficult to be precise on what a 'case' is because it is a word that, across disciplines, has different emphases. He describes the interpretation of Louis Smith, an early education ethnographer, who saw viewing the case as a 'bounded system' as helpful. It is an object rather than a process, so the case is:

> . . . *an integrated system. The parts do not have to be working well, the parts may be irrational, but it is a system. Thus people and programs are clearly the prospective cases.* (Stake 1996:2)

The focus moves towards understanding the detail and complexities revealed by an examination of a person or group of people in a specific context or situation. A case may be a service user, a group of service users, or even a staff team.

A case study can often be about insights on the ordinary, hearing a person's story, an oral history, finding pieces of a picture that normally would not be heard or seen or understood. It allows for a detailed examination of a specific event or group of events and their connective parts.

It infers a narrow scope of quality and depth, gathering many small and significant threads which together form a focused whole. This whole might help, for example, an organisation to understand what the implementation of a particular policy might mean for an individual service user or group of staff.

Service users involvement in research

In all areas of the human services there is an increasing emphasis on involving service users in decision-making, often acting out 'pretended partnerships' that are stated rather than felt. There also is a growing wealth of books that allow marginalised voices to be heard in an authentic and less diluted fashion than formal systems often allow for. Case studies enable you be concerned with returning to the basics of listening and learning about others, and in doing so hopefully understanding more about both professional and private selves.

Stake (1996:91) argues that in case research, the researcher will construct a role for themselves that may be one or a combination of the following:

teacher	storyteller	evaluator
participant observer	advocate	consultant
interviewer	counsellor	others
reader		

This infers that the role is constructed by the individual researcher and the subjects of the case study. Deliberately or sub-consciously the researcher takes up a role particular to each case study. Sheehan, in describing her route to writing about foster care, shows one type of relationship for a case study approach:

> *They (social workers) said she was articulate, would enjoy being written about and would stay the course . . . She agreed to work with me 'it'd probably kinda help me learn my roots' she said – and did indeed stay the course, a two-and-a-half year one, with unfailing veracity and high spirits.* (Sheehan, 1993)

For this journalistic endeavour the interviewer/storyteller role, carried out with integrity and respect, appeared to fit the needs of both parties involved.

Reflexivity in case study research

The type of subjectivity of the case study approach, as in the example above, has been criticised. For the research-learner, ensuring quality means grappling with this criticism as an ongoing dimension of the work. It involves being aware of how you as a person, with your own values, knowledge and personality, for example, will influence the information that is gathered and how you interpret that information.

The following questions may exemplify the type of questions you might ask of yourself at any stage in the research:

- Can you as a researcher actually see that one event can have a number of interpretations?
- How is your experience or outlook affecting the way you build the picture of the case study you are looking at?
- By being aware of different realities, how can this help you to convey some kind of consensual truth, for instance one that is agreed by the researcher and research subjects?

Sanger (1996:6), gives a reminder of the need for researchers to keep questioning their motives and the reality they construct for themselves in particular moments:

> . . . *information is that which an individual perceives as significant.*

Calling an activity 'research', does not automatically lend it some objective dimension. It is still you at your workplace, perhaps asking a different question and looking in new places for the answer. It is not possible to hide or deny the clouded view you bring to the case study. So own it and use it to help you analyse what is going on.

How can case study analysis help you learn

Case study analysis is a tool for learning because it requires a challenging of the habitual expectations that are brought to situations and which inform an analysis of an event.

In working with particular groups of service users, perhaps having similar needs, your practice present is framed by what Ostrow (1990:24) describes as 'pre-reflexivity'. Existing practical and theoretical knowledge is mediated by 'filters through which we interpret the world' (Hope and Pickles, 1995) and which in turn mediate responses to new situations and people.

Professional community, youth or social workers may talk about treating people as individuals and feel that they are doing so. Undertaking a case study analysis means stopping and checking out the state of your own filters and whether they are in fact blocking new insights.

In gathering hard information about a situation from the people involved for case study research, there is an opportunity to be exposed to perceptions you may take for granted, as well as a chance to rethink strategies to improve your development or that of your organisation.

The example below illustrates the blocks that can build up.

Mary's experience

As part of a monitoring exercise I asked Open University students I was working with for their perceptions of the support I had given them. One student fed back how unsupported she had felt. This was a student I had given more time to than

---

> any other on the course by a considerable margin, and for whom extra learning support had also been provided. I had set out my view of the role of tutor early in the course but had not checked out with students how they defined 'support'. I realised that I had brought a 'taken-for-granted' view about support to this group of students that did not match their own views. This mismatch then affected the quality of the learning experience, certainly for that student.

Case study analysis may help to create the space that is often hard to find to look in detail at routine work with people.

Problem-based approaches

Defining a problem

Problem-based enquiry or learning means taking seriously the issues that arise in the day-to-day business of practice. Robinson (1993:25) describes a problem as 'a gap between an existing and desired state of affairs'.

This frames a problem as something with negative connotations. Robinson (1993) goes on to suggest an alternative view that is more helpful and neutral in that a problem can be seen as 'a puzzle or challenge that needs to be resolved'.

For the action researcher this certainly presents an approach that is less likely to be threatening to colleagues and others in the workplace. It recognises that by its very nature practice is puzzling and that exploring such puzzles is a positive sign of a learning culture.

Robinson (1993) describes problem-solving as a way of understanding better the constraints that stop the achievement of certain organisational objectives. These may be experienced in a very personal way.

For the practitioner looking to build a learner-outlook more explicitly into their work it is often the identification of a problem that will trigger the necessary curiosity to act upon the need for more learning. As Lovell (1980:66) says:

> *Not until the problem is defined does it really exist in a form that is capable of solution then what we really need to do is explore the field in which the problem exists.*

Individual and collective approaches to problem-solving

Some organisations may set up problem-based teams, often cross-departmental or cross-functional, to explore quality issues and service development. These may also be called *quality circles* (Reece and Brandt, 1996:315).

You may also have experience of problem-based learning in education or training. This also tends to focus upon group learning as a way of tackling issues that present strategic options. Both these activities may ring bells from Chapter 4's discussion of working parties and professional development groups.

There are many advantages to working on problem resolution using a collective approach such as cross-fertilisation of ideas and building collective ownership of the problem as well as the solution. For a number of reasons, however, such shared opportunities for problem-solving may not always be accessible or sufficient for dealing with a problem you identify.

By using a problem-based approach to a research question individuals may be able to:

> *... conceive solutions to the problems with a degree of clarity that escapes them in the rush and clutter of their day-to-day lives.* (Stringer (1996:97)

Winning the support of others to tackle the problem

The action researcher who is interested in problem-solving needs to win over other people who have a stake in possible solutions, people who can be identified as 'stakeholders'. These may be:

Research stakeholders

- service users
- colleagues
- managers
- management or steering committees
- policy makers
- agency partners
- community (of shared interest or a locality-based community)

It is no good attempting to question or tackle a problem if others around you do not also see the issue as a problem. An action research stance places you in a position of research *facilitator* (Stringer, 1996). Your project will be doomed if you do not do your early groundwork in checking out that people are prepared to explore the issue with you.

At such a stage a danger is that people want to talk about lots of perceived problems. It may well be that there are interconnected issues but often in practitioner research a key function is containing the scale of the task. Better to try out and achieve a short, small piece of work than attempt something that becomes unwieldy and unfocused. Robinson (1996:115) argues that problem-based methodology should include a reflective dimension as a way of accounting for *the reasoning that informs critical decisions in qualitative research*.

Pragmatism in problem-solving

The focus of the discussion in looking at case study analysis was on the subjective dynamics it may generate. A problem-based approach as a functional activity can also effect change and make positive improvements.

Problem-based research, if carried out with good planning and using action research principles, offers a practical way for practitioners to link individual to organisational learning. Motivation is provided by the possibility of doing something that aims to have a tangible impact on performance or policies. The learner-researcher is helped in their sense-making by other stakeholders in the research project. To address a thorny issue effectively in an organisational context requires stakeholders and researcher to take account of a number of elements.

Stakeholders need to:

- Be clear about the purpose of the research task.
- Understand how and when information will be collected.
- Know who will see the information and how it will be presented.
- Be consulted about change to any of the above.
- Be committed to enabling change if the research outcomes suggest improvements are needed.

Researchers need to:

- Be able to work co-operatively with other stakeholders.
- Protect themselves by ensuring communication lines are clear and decisions are recorded accurately.
- Do what has been agreed with other stakeholders.
- Discuss with stakeholders or their representatives before making changes, or agree a short cut if urgent decisions need to be made.
- Assist stakeholders in linking the research results to change possibilities.
- Have support and honesty from management and those with responsibility for change implementation, and that the task, if agreed, is not tokenised. i.e. build in an action element to the outcomes.

As with all learning research involves a cycle of:

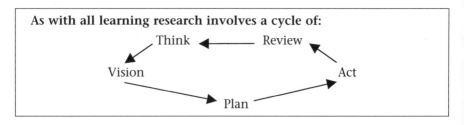

An example of the planning stages for a small-scale action research project

Introduction

This final section includes an example of how a small-scale action research project might be carried out in an agency. This will:

- Reiterate key messages and principles concerned with action research.
- Show how a project might move forward from an idea, through to planning, implementation and review.

The example is set out to illustrate a problem-based approach and provides contextual information and makes explicit the issues and questions that arise during planning stages.

The agency

A voluntary sector agency set up to deliver community-based prevention programmes for young people (aged 11–17) at risk of offending/reoffending.

Staffing

The agency has:

- 1 full-time manager (social work trained)
- 1 full-time project worker
- 3 part-time project workers (with a variety of backgrounds, including one ex-teacher and a trainee youth worker undertaking a qualifying course)
- 1 part-time administrator
- volunteers, including young people, for help with specific programmes

Funding

It receives core funding from an inter-agency partnership of education, social service and youth service, and also grant funding focused on specific programmes. There is an inter-agency Development Group with representatives of these and other agencies to maintain links, discuss programme issues and ongoing funding.

Community context

The agency operates in a county town in a rural area. There are pockets of social deprivation on two older housing developments, most of which are still rented from a housing association, and the population is largely indigenous and of white British origin. Unemployment amongst young people aged 16–24 is relatively high and there is more movement away from the area amongst this age group than other population age bands.

The programmes

The agency focuses on two programmes for the 11–14 age group:

- After-school and holiday activities on the two older housing developments offering constructive use of leisure time and focusing on providing 'high energy' appeal.
- In-school programme for boys only, operating on a referral basis, and focused on issues such as anger management, risky behaviour and assertiveness.

For the 15–17 age group there are also two programmes:

Mentoring scheme—for young people who have been cautioned by the police and who are considered to be at risk of a final warning. Mentoring support is offered as an option. Mentors are volunteers who provide a positive adult role model, give support, provide access to information, and accompany the young person on a contracted programme of activities lasting between two and six months

Citizenship project—developing wider participation by young people in a range of community and social issues e.g. workshops in schools, working with established groups to enable them to project their needs to local decision-makers (called 'Ideas to Action'), developing a world wide web site with and for young people on community issues and action.

The question

One of the part-time female project workers, Amanda, who worked on the citizenship project, thought she identified a pattern amongst the 'Ideas to Action' groups that there was less active involvement by young men . She was not sure if this was actually an accurate view but after mulling it over in her mind for a while she came up with the following question:

Do the young men and women who are part of 'Ideas to Action' want similar things from being involved?

Rather than posing a question about the involvement itself Amanda felt it would be more helpful to take a step further back to address the issue. If there were differences in the motivations of young people for getting involved, this would probably impact on the type or level of participation.

If she asked a question about the participation of boys only this might wrongly assume that the starting points of young men and women are the same. She remembered her youth work training creed of 'start from where young people are' and this is what she wanted her question to do.

So what to do with her question?

Amanda did a few things before she moved her question into a research activity.

1. She talked informally with her colleagues and some young people from 'Ideas in Action' to see whether her question seemed a valid or real one to them.
2. She talked to her manager about the question during supervision and explained she wanted to look at it a bit more closely as she felt this might influence how to work more effectively with young men and young women.
3. She raised the question at a team meeting and asked if other people felt it might be worth looking at more closely.

This revealed different perspectives:

- Some people had thought about gender issues, but had not pinned it down to how young people participated.
- Some people did think that there were gender differences, others did not.
- Most people across the group liked the idea of doing some sort of research on the programme.

A shift away from 'my' question to 'our' problem. Thus from being a tentative question, Amanda's initial thinking gradually evolved into 'a practice issue' for the agency.

Practical implications

With the endorsement of colleagues and her manager Amanda was able to turn her question into an action plan. She was given two hours per week workload relief for six weeks to find some sort of response to her question, with some conditions attached. She knew that whilst it was good to get the endorsement of her line manager she would also have to spend time at home working on the project.

Amanda's line manager would act as supervisor for the research, and also suggested a member of the development group, Gerry, who was familiar with research and who would be able to give her advice and support, could act in a coaching capacity. Her older sister who was studying for a social sciences degree was able to act as an informal mentor.

The objectives were defined as:

- To produce a short report in writing at a team meeting (with a date).
- To feedback to the young people in 'Ideas in Action' on findings and conclusions in an accessible format (within a named period of time):
  –verbal presentation
  –leaflet
  –news item for the web page done in the style of an interview by a young person
- To involve young people in the research with their permission.

Preparing for the research

Amanda now had to move her question into another stage of planning.

She wanted the research activities to be reflective of youth work values and this meant putting the following principles first:

- valuing the young people
- involving them at a level suited to their needs
- being open
- respecting their views
- working with them in partnership

Limitations

She recognised there were limitations she needed to consider in designing her project:

- **Time-scale**—the work had to be completed within six weeks
- **Resources**—time to give to the project would be limited to two hours at work and probably three hours at home per week.
- **Funding**—none was available (e.g. for room hire or travel), so the research activities had to fit in with the usual programme.
- **Computer**—the agency had one, but no survey programme.
- **Skills**—Gerry from the development group could help with advice but Amanda had not done research except for college work.

Strengths and opportunities

Remember the SLOT analysis from Chapter 3. In designing the research it was important for Amanda to recognise the current skills she brought to the task and also areas she felt less confident about. She identified current strengths as:

- an existing positive relationship with the young people
- good interpersonal skills such as listening and group-work
- willingness to learn
- good organisational skills
- competent on a p.c.

However her knowledge of statistical research methods and 'number crunching' might lead to a loss of productivity.

Amanda recognised that the research offered the chance for personal development and identified the following outcomes she hoped for as a result of doing the work:

- more confidence in undertaking research
- increased competence in the linking of research data and findings to action

- more understanding of how to work in a proactive way with gender differences in youth work

The first two outcomes were related to the activities she would be doing. The third was related primarily to the research findings but also to her ability to be reflexive in her encounters with young people and adults when doing the research. She could observe and be self-aware about the dynamics of those encounters to learn from for the future.

Next she talked to Gerry about:

- resource issues
- context issues
- personal capacities and development needs

Amanda set out her plan for the six week project, working backwards and dividing the time available into stages.

Methods of data collection

As Amanda knew that this timetable only gave modest leeway to allow for a small delays at any stage of the work, she had to plan to use methodologies that were realistic for this time-scale.

A conversation with Gerry encouraged her to consider the following questions:

- what information do I need to know?
- who is the information for?
- what will happen to the information?
- how will it be presented?
- who or where can I find this information from?
- what options do I have for getting this information?
- which options will best suit the time-scale and resources of the project?
- which information do I need first?
- and crucially, what am I in all this?

It was vital for Amanda to hold on to a conscious awareness of having three roles.

She was working for her employer as a **practitioner** *and* undertaking a task that brought with it the temporary role of **researcher** *and* she saw this opprtunity as a chance to be a **learner** of new skills and insights.

What are the problems of this multi-purpose role for the research?

Stake (1995:103) identifies a number of choices the person in this position might need to make in what he calls 'case researcher roles'. He suggests the researcher needs to make an honest and ethical choice about the interpretation of the role they take up.

For Amanda her choice might have involved:

- How she presented her data collection, either as part of her work or as a discrete activity with an alternative purpose.
- How to use her existing relationship with the young people, but not abuse or manipulate it. She needed to discuss with them what she wanted to do and ensure they wanted to take part as it was outside the normal programme activities.

To assist her with thinking through the ethical and practical issues Gerry had lent Amanda a book on research methods and she had also visited her local library to get some books on:

- data-collection methods
- doing research with young people
- existing research about gender issues, citizenship and young people

At first she felt overwhelmed by all the information but by staying focused on the specifics of her piece of work she was able to identify an appropriate approach. She also found books on gender differences as background reading and spent several hours surfing the web using key words like citizenship and youth.

Decision-making about methods of data-collection

She realised she needed to use an approach that would not have a long lead-in time and that would not generate huge amounts of work in collating data. Linked to her SLOT analysis of the situations she decided upon:

No self-administered questionnaires—not appropriate for the group, not enough young people to make a survey significant and preparation may take too long.

No taped interviews—would take too long to transcribe (don't be fooled by using tapes as any kind of short cut; a one hour tape can take about three hours to transcribe).

She opted for a combination of three ways of collecting data.

1. Looking at records from the project and collating data to compare information on young men and women involved in 'Ideas in Action'. Records could tell Amanda:

- ages
- length of involvement
- profile of the different 'Ideas in Action' groups (seven altogether)
- staff involved in each group

2. Guided discussions with current groups from 'Ideas in Action':

- Split into single sex groups.

- Focused upon generating discussion about motivations and interests in being involved including how they heard about the group.
- Having a non-participant write up key points on a flipchart during the discussion, so the data to be used was clear for everyone in the room to see and agree.

3. Semi-structured interviews with staff and volunteers involved in 'Ideas in Action':

- Done individually, as it proved too difficult to arrange a group interview due to existing commitments.
- Using a proforma filled out during the interview and shown to each staff member for approval.

Plans for data collation

For data collation from the first activity, using existing records, Amanda set up a grid to record her information for each group as shown below and recorded the information straight on to the computer in the office. This meant a maximum of seven sides of A4.

For the second and third data collection activities she planned to collate the data straight from the paperwork used in the interviews.

Group name				Number of young people in group	
Staff involved					
Type of setting					
Action focus of the group					
Name of young person	Gender	Age	Length of involvement	Reasons for joining (if known)	Things they did in the group

Figure 1. Form for collating information from existing '*Ideas in Action*' records.

With planning completed Amanda could get on and **do** the research project!

References

Ashton, A. (1998) Evidence-based Practice, *SSRG Newsletter*, November 1998.

Alasuutari, P (1995) *Researching Culture—Qualitative Method and Cultural Studies*, London: Sage.

Atkins, M.J. (1984) Practitioner as Researcher: Some Techniques for Analysing Semi-structured Data for Small-scale Research, *British Journal of Educational Studies*, Vol XXX11 No 3 October 1984, pp. 251–261.

Bell, M. (1987) *Doing Your Research Project—A Guide for First Time Researchers in Education and Social Sciences*, Milton Keynes: Open University Press.

Denscombe, M. (1998) *The Good Research Guide*, Buckingham: OU Press.

Edwards, A. and Talbot, R. (1994) *The Hard-pressed Researcher: A Research Handbook for the Caring Professions*, New York, Longman.

Friedman, B. (1998) *The Research Tool Kit—Putting it all Together*, Pacific Grove: Brooks/Cole Publishing Company.

Fuller, R. and Petch, A. (1995) *Practitioner Research, The Reflexive Social Worker*, Buckingham: Open University Press.

Hawtin, M., Hughes, G. and Percy-Smith, J. (1994) *Community Profiling Auditing Social Needs*, Buckingham: Open University Press.

Hope, P. and Pickles, T. (1995) *Performance Appraisal: A Handbook for Managers in Public and Voluntary Organisations*, Lyme Regis: Russell House Publishing Ltd..

Lovell, Bernard R. (1980) *Adults Learning*, London: Croom Helm.

National Extension College (1992) *Techniques of Investigation an Introduction to Research Methods*, Cambridge: NEC.

Ostrow, J. (1990) *Social Sensitivity—A Study of Habit and Experience*, Albany: State University of New York Press.

Reece, B. and Brandt, R. (1996 6th edition) *Effective Human Relations in Organisations*, Boston: Houghton Mufflin Company.

Robinson, V. (1993) *Problem-based Methodology*, Oxford: Pergamon Press.

Sanger, J. (1996) *The Complete Observer? A Fixed Research Guide to Observation*, London: Falmer Press.

Sheehan, S. (1993) *Life for me ain't been no Crystal Stair*, New York: Vintage Books.

Stake, R.T. (1995) *The Art of Case Study Research*, Thousand Oaks: Sage.

Stringer, T. (1996) *Action Research—A Handbook for Practitioners*, Thousand Oaks: Sage.

Winter, R. (1996) Some Principles and Procedures for the Conduct of Action Research in Zuber-Skeritt, O. (Ed.) *New Directions in Action Research*, London: Falmer Press.

Zuber-Skeritt, O. (Ed.) (1996) *New Directions in Action Research*, London: Falmer Press.

Zuber-Skeritt, O. (1996) Emancipatory Action Research for Organisational Change and Management Development in Zuber-Skeritt, O. (Ed.) *New Directions in Action Research*, London: Falmer Press

7. Learning pathways and professional development

> Would you tell me please which way I ought to go from here?
> That depends a good deal on where you want to get to, said the Cat.
> I don't much care where, said Alice.
> Then it doesn't matter which way you go, said the Cat.
> Lewis Carroll, 'Alice's Adventures in Wonderland'

Having looked at practical ideas and activities, the book concludes with an overview of the social and policy contexts that may influence learning at work. The chapter is divided into four sections and each one addresses a theme related to contemporary learning issues for adults at work.

Learning pathways

Learners today face a dilemma of choice. If you are thinking about options for work-based education or training you may feel as though you are entering a wood in which there are many paths going in different directions but no map to guide you. As the above quote illustrates if *you* know where you're going then you know what route to look for.

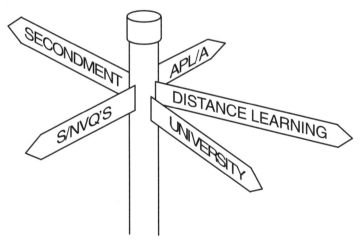

Figure 1. Signpost.

You may have many questions about how particular learning or development opportunities can meet your learning needs and career goals:

- What on-the-job training is available?
- What is an S/NVQ?
- Will employers recognise my S/NVQ?
- Is my S/NVQ too specific to use in another job?
- Can I combine an academic programme with work?
- Is an academic programme going to help me do my job better?
- Can I make all the in-house training days and courses I have done for my employer count towards any qualification?
- How much time does a post-qualification portfolio take to produce?

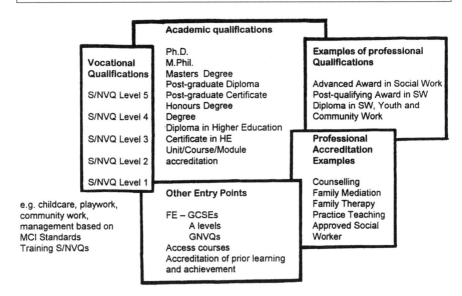

Boxes show work towards a seamless approach, with options for joint awards growing.

Figure 2. Types of qualifications.

The widening of options in learning opportunities can be a hindrance and act as a smokescreen rather than a help when a choice needs to be made. This problem has not gone unnoticed by policy makers. As Fryer (1997:6) notes:

> ... *funders, providers and awarding bodies should all address the urgent need to reduce the complexity, eliminate unnecessary bureaucracy and red tape, cut out duplication and simplify progression routes, qualifications and learning pathways.*

This streamlining indicates a need for institutions and systems to adapt to the needs of learners rather than the other way around. This view is supported by a Minister of Lifelong Learning, who stated (Kingston, P. 1999:13):

We have as a department to give as much attention to the community and to people in work as we have to people within the formal education system . . . The notion of simply expecting people to come tripping into city centre middle-class colleges is noodle-headed.

Part of the solution to the issue of choice involves widening access to include up to date and accurate information, advice and guidance. You may be lucky and have a training manager or someone else at your work who can answer all your questions.

Other people and organisations that can help include:

- Careers guidance services and private careers counsellors.
- Your local Training and Enterprise Council.
- Professional bodies—such as the National Youth Agency, CCETSW (soon to be disbanded and superceded by the General Social Care Council)
- Trade Unions – Community and Youth Workers Union, British Association of Social Work, National Association of Probation Officers.
- Training officers or managers at your organisation's head office if you have one, or an organisation to which yours is affiliated.
- Direct from colleges, universities, training providers or awarding bodies and government funded bodies such as the Qualifications and Curriculum Authority or the Department for Education and Employment.
- From the world wide web – the web sites of groups listed above or specialist sites – key in words such as 'education + guidance + adults' e.g. http://www.youth.org.uk, http://www.prospects.csu.man.ac.uk, http://www.cando.lancs.ac.uk—a site supporting disabled graduates.
- Public libraries.
- Telephone helplines such as *Learning Direct* (0800 100 900).

An employment pathway in youth and social care work

Arguably an employment feature of youth and community work and also the health and social care field is the transition many people make from service user to service provider. A decision to take up paid work may be made as a result of experience as a user of a service in the local community. At this stage the thought of formal or higher education may seem very distant. Many roles in health, welfare and community work are, simply, chanced upon.

A simplified career pathway outlines how many people enter the field.

> service user
>> ⇨ volunteer
>>> ⇨ paid sessional work
>>>> ⇨ professional training
>>>>> ⇨ employment as a qualified practitoner

With minor variations, this reflects the author's own pathway into youth work. Organisations like Youth Clubs UK use this type of progression as a framework for the development of young people, for example within their Youth Achievements Awards (Youth Clubs UK, 1999).

It may not be until the third stage of paid work that the scope of work possibilities becomes clearer. Many users of therapeutic residential services aspire to become drug or alcohol counsellors. A focus may develop, not because it is really the best choice, but because proper guidance about other related or different options has not been available.

An issue facing many learners is how to access impartial and detailed guidance with which they can make an informed choice about employment and associated education or training pathways. The list given earlier shows that there are many sources of help. Guidance is not a one-off activity, and can assist at many different stages of a career, for example:

- after a career break looking after children or other dependant relatives
- if an illness, disability or criminal conviction necessitates a change
- due to redundancy
- move to a new area or country
- if different opportunities present and you have to decide on the best option

A 1999 government consultation paper sets out the value placed on guidance for the expanding number of today's lifelong learners:

> *The Government recognises that these increases in participation will have a significant impact on the demand from individuals for information about learning opportunities and for advice and guidance about what is right for them. The availability of good quality information, advice and guidance can also have a critical role in encouraging people, particularly the socially disadvantaged and disabled people, to become involved in learning and to improve their prospects in the labour market.* (DfEE, 1999)

People often want to make their experience count and to know that an investment of time and energy in training will pay off. Requirements for entry, and assessments for training and education programmes are constantly changing, and it is inappropriate, therefore, to attempt to offer specific information here. There is, then a diversity of current opportunities and guidance available to assist you in decision-making and finding your own answers to your needs.

The learning divide

Although learning opportunities are increasing it is also true that access to these opportunities is not always equal. Social inequalities do not get left behind when you are at work, as this section will go on to show. Debates about access that have informed the rise of new training qualifications are also discussed.

It is not uncommon, for example, for the most qualified parts of the workforce to get best access to continuing professional development. A study by Blundell et al. (1996:69), exploring work-related training in Britain concluded that:

> . . . the returns to training were found to be complementary with formal education, but the highest returns were found to accrue to those with only intermediate levels of education. This group is of particular interest since we have also shown that they are relatively less likely to be receiving training in comparison with the more highly educated workers in Britain. They also appear to get less training than similarly educated workers in Germany and the US.

So whilst the least educated are the most likely to miss out on traditional training opportunities, they are often the group that benefit the most in terms of wage increases when they do access middle or higher vocational qualifications. Blundell's study looked at two types of training:

- employer-provided training courses and
- work-related training leading to a formal vocational qualification (both in-house and externally provided)

The problem of giving a universal definition to the term 'training' is recognised by the authors of the study but some patterns emerge (Blundell et al., 1996:9):

- males have better access to training than females
- training decreases with age
- minority groups have a lower probability of receiving training
- part-time workers receive less training than full-time workers
- union members receive more training than non-members
- higher education qualifications raise the probability of receiving training
- training probability is lower when unemployment is high

These patterns provide a clear indication that social disadvantage and exclusion do not confine themselves to the realms of private life but impact directly on opportunities for personal and career development.

Although critics of National Vocational Qualifications focus upon their reductionist possibilities it is worth noting that the 1981 Department of Employment Report, *New Training Initiative*, that paved their way, highlighted issues of access (Jessup, 1989:65, Wolf, 1995:7). There was a concern about huge sections of the workforce being kept out of the qualifications and vocational education and training market. Jessup (1989:67) cites the following barriers to work-related training:

- having special needs
- age limits
- regulations regarding specified periods of experience or training
- constraints of learning modes and course structures

The development of standards linked to competency frameworks is seen by Wolf (1995:7) as influenced by reformers whose concern was to:

> . . . *open up access, especially for 'non-traditional learners', and their dislike was not for unions but for educational establishments which they felt to be overly academic, self-interested, elitist, and a bar to equal opportunity.*

Advocates of the new system felt that traditional education and training systems put the providers' interests first whereas the new approach intended to put the learner or candidate at the centre.

This view needs, of course, to be tempered against the issue of qualifications versus standards as highlighted in Chapters 2 and 3. The occupational standards upon which S/NVQs are based, are driven by the need for service and business improvement. The individual benefits of qualifications can in some ways been seen as secondary to these organisational and occupational group benefits.

Indeed the widespread individual benefits anticipated do not appear to have impacted as widely in the workplace as might be hoped. For as Fryer reports (1997:2):

> *The Labour Force Survey regularly finds only 14 per cent of all employees taking part in job-related training and while the National Advisory Council for Education and Training reports real progress in recent years, one third of all employees say that their employer has never offered them any kind of training.*
>
> *Only 5 per cent of the workforce have so far obtained an S/NVQ and two thirds of organisations employing 50 people or more have not yet even made a commitment to try to achieve the Investors in People standard.*

The Qualifications and Curriculum Authority (QCA) says that from its own statistics 42 per cent of the UK workforce are with an employer using S/NVQs (Reith, 1998:22).

In 1999 the National Advisory Group for Continuing Education and Lifelong Learning recommended that there was still much to do to gear learning to the rhythms of the workplace, particularly with small employers (NAGCELL, 1999).

It is also the case that the response to competence-based systems in many sectors has been varied, with a great deal of scepticism towards their introduction in some occupational areas. The ten years since the inception of S/NVQs shows the attitudinal shifts, partly informed by the revisions to the standards and assessment procedures themselves. Reith (1998:22) cites a DfEE spokesperson who commented:

> . . . *it took eight years to reach the first million (certificates awarded) and only another three years to reach the second million.*

Social work and youth work has been critical of competence-based approaches. The following quote encapsulates sharply some of the key criticisms:

> *As the shift to pseudo-objective, mechanistic and narrow task-centred notions of 'competences' with which it was already flirting has gathered pace, youth and community work training has become even further detached from its adult education base.* (Norton et al., 1994:22)

The replacement culture 'which promotes market forces, consumerism and managerialism' (Lishman, 1998:89) is seen as anathema to many practitioners.

A common misconception about S/NVQs are that they are training qualifications. They are not training programmes but are concerned with demonstrations of competence within a particular role (Fletcher, 1997, Braye and Preston-Shoot, 1996, Eraut, 1994) derived from occupational standards.

The overlaying of S/NVQs onto a professional qualification, however, has presented many concerns as mentioned above. These include:

- Reductionism within a system that emphasises behaviourist outcomes (competencies).
- Corresponding failure in early versions of standards in particular to incorporate professional values and ethics.
- Difficulty with accommodating contextual issues and the impact of the different assessment environments S/NVQ candidates work in.
- Introspection and narrowness—assessors may often be managers and 'the standard' expected in one organisation may be higher or lower than in another.
- Lack of confidence in the rigour of the assessment processes.
- Concern about differential detail and requirements across different S/NVQs

but judged to be of the same level. Is a Level 1 in community work the same as a Care S/NVQ at Level 1?

- Concern about the consultation processes and time-scales within which standards were developed and implemented, which by default mitigated against a genuinely democratic consultation process.

Yet even whilst anti-competence debates raged, the new standards were opening up training and qualifications to many unqualified social care staff. A report by the Social Care Association on the professional needs of those working with children in residential care highlights the increased attention:

Any investment of this sort is a welcome development, especially as many of the workforce will previously have had no significant training at all (Lane, 1999:8).

Lane argues that there needs to be a sustained investment in training, however, and that providing S/NVQ Level 3 for residential child care workers should be viewed as a beginning, not an end.

One of the divisions in the debates about vocational qualifications is their comparative value to academic qualifications. The value ascribed to vocational qualifications varies amongst employers and organisations. S/NVQs may assist people in stepping onto a career ladder but there may be missing rungs for further advancement. The route to qualification for Probation Officers is one example combining a joint vocational and academic approach. This integrated model incorporating work-based learning looks set to expand.

As Payne (1999) says:

a middle way, which integrates competence and reflective learning, seems to be emerging. (p. 54)

Lifelong learning

Lifelong learning is a term that it has been adopted by many groups but with a variety of meanings. Song Seng and Sock Hwee (1997:1) provide the following definition:

Lifelong learning, in its broadest sense, is the continuation of any and all forms of learning through one's life. It encompasses adult education, vocational skills acquisition and other less formal activities that contribute to the social well-being and personal development of the individual. However, increasingly lifelong learning is viewed as an essential capability in a people, workforce and society in order to compete successfully in a global economy.

For Larsson (1997:251) this shift means that 'lifelong learning risks losing its richness and precision as a concept'. He views lifelong learning as more person-centred and holistic, as it:

- involves changed realities and interpretations
- includes development of action as an important part of learning
- sees the reflective process as central to the two dimensions above

This focus on the personal change dimensions of learning fits with the learner-outlook theme of the book. Increasingly, however, individual learning is defined within the broader context of the learning organisation. Continuing professional development is entwined with notions of quality and competence.

Watson (1992:159), sees this as as positive in that it addresses the complacency that may be engendered by a one-off professional qualification. Evidence of continuing professional learning is an integral part of the profile of the employable practitioner or manager. Yet Fryer (1997:1) notes that in the general population:

only one adult in four describes themselves as a current learner, and one in three has taken no part in education or training since leaving school.

This indicates the scale of the task involved in enabling people to reshape their thinking to see learning as part of their day-to-day routine; to identify with a learner-outlook as a way of viewing working life. Learning continues to be seen by some people as separate and distinct from experience and the ordinary.

An example of change triggering a review of needs is provided by a social work practitioner of many years experience who had recently moved to the voluntary sector from the statutory sector. She described the problem she had identified at work of finding 'space for intellectual freedom'.

She was aware of sliding into 'doing without thinking' mode and was searching for a way of holding onto the critical perspective she felt was essential to her identity as a professional social worker. The priorities of her employing agency put the need for critical debate well below the pragmatic priorities of working towards targets and monitoring outcomes. *Process* issues appeared tangential to the core business of the agency. She was seeking a learning or developmental opportunity that would fill this void for her, even if her agency was not supportive of these learning needs.

Hopefully, most people working in the human services will be part of a work culture that sees personal development as an integral component of quality standards in their organisation. There is a tension, however, as mentioned earlier in the book, which is concerned with the balance between personal learning needs versus those of the employer. There may be peaks of awareness about these learning needs created by:

- attendance on a formal programme of learning
- periods of self-examination, perhaps when considering role or job changes
- triggers from internal or external factors such as quality reviews and inspections

The profile of lifelong learning in the UK was raised following publication of the DfEE's consultation paper, *The Learning Age—A Renaissance for a New Britain* (1998). The report sees lifelong learning as one strategic arm for achieving social change. Learning is held up as the means by which cultural unification and economic prosperity will come about. It is an ambitious document and attempts to address the issues of lifelong learning as they affect:

- individuals
- businesses
- communities
- the nation

It defines lifelong learning as:

> ... *the continuous development of the skills, knowledge and understanding that are essential for employability and fulfilment.*

The balance of the recommendations appear in reality to be channelled towards the economy, and having an appropriately skilled and trained workforce to cope with the changing face of the employment market.

Explicitly and implicitly, therefore, workplace learning in this context represents both a way of balancing the inequality of access to new skills and also the culture that employers and businesses need to develop to keep them competitive.

Different priorities are identified in *The Learning Age* paper for achieving this vision. Those that seem to be particularly relevant to workplace learners include:

- Using new technologies to support learning in a variety of environments.
- Increasing the range and flexibility of learning opportunities for individual learners.
- Promoting portfolio learning to include the management of individual learning accounts that enable people to purchase their own learning support at appropriate times in their working life.
- Addressing the current inequalities of access to, and participation in, learning opportunities.
- Creating a simplified pathway through different education and training qualifications.
- Enabling and supporting learning businesses.

Vocationalism continues to be the developmental model favoured for realising this culture. Although knowledge is encompassed in the definition, and the role of higher education is discussed, it is **skills** acquisition that dominates the vision.

The Learning Age paper appears to encourage all stakeholders in the learning process to consider the barriers and opportunities for flexible learning and looks to both individuals and organisations.

Workplace learning into the 21st century

Developing the role and nature of workplace learning is one of a number of contemporary change initiatives to learning and standards frameworks at national level. Reviews of social work education, youth work National Occupational Standards (NOS), the demise of the Social Work Education and Training Council (DOH, 1999, NYA, 1999 [2]) all indicate the vigour in the intention to map what is distinctive about each occupational area and where there is convergence with others. Different bodies now have responsibility for the development of vocational qualifications as National Training Organisations (NTOs) in each occupational are and the NOS upon which they are based. For example there will be a new NTO for the Personal Social Services (ESWIN, 1999).

Work continues to identify the way activities and qualifications across the different types of social care, youth, community, criminal justice and early years work, for example, can fit together to represent the full range of roles that workers undertake. In the workplace activities will increasingly be defined and measured against the NOS as well as local requirements. Learning opportunities and staff development will continue to focus upon attaining and sustaining these standards. Even those working in small or isolated settings can be part of a framework that will be common to other organisations doing the same type of work.

National Learning Targets for England for 2002 were set by the DfEE (DfEE, 1999) to follow through the commitment to its learning initiatives. Another of these that focuses upon learning at work is the University of Industry.

A direction for learning at work has emerged that requires:

• Employers to implement a learning culture with supportive resources.
• Learners to have a sense of ownership in the reshaping of sites of learning.

The role assigned by the government for the University for Industry is to address the two areas that are irrevocably entwined with employment:

• the UK skills shortage
• social exclusion issues

Employers want to have more control of their learning supplies and suppliers. The DfEE (1998b2:1) cites connectivity as one of the university's key qualities:

It will help connect people and businesses who want to learn with ways of doing so, and plug gaps in the supply of learning.

One of the most powerful resources that the university will have on hand to assist with utilising existing best practice and stimulating new initiatives is harnessing the unprecedented range and power of technologies available today.

The speed of technological advancement is sometimes hard to grasp, not least because of the size of the information highway that can now be travelled. Digital television, for example, has now entered private homes. Anticipation rather than realisation of the potential of this new technology for learning exists at the time of writing. Keying in and almost immediately being able to watch a learning programme of choice seems an age away from the origins of open learning programming. Yet when introduced it was revolutionary in its own way.

Frissen (1997), in a critique of informatisation and its effect on public administration, argues that the information and communications technologies (ICTs) require us to consider economies of scope instead of economies of scale.

The territorial issues that are rendered obsolete by electronic connections are creating possibly greater inter-organisational communication than intra-organisational. Frissen (1997:113), puts the effects even more strongly when he says:

. . . these electronic connections may become more important than the physical organisations and organisational units they connect. Societal and policy networks or configurations can effectively be represented in electronic networks. Cyberspace is the 'real' space.

This has led to what Frissen describes as 'the horizontalisation of relations'. This flattening of hierarchies must not be mistaken for 'equality' of relations, however. Mechanisms and processes of domination are as active in cyberspace as in other arenas of human communication. Only a few steps have been taken into the moral maze of responsible usage of electronic communication.

It is speculative to anticipate the potential of the new technologies to tackle the divisions of access to education and training for different staff groups in the workplace. For employers the choices of models of delivery of training in the workplace are growing. As is emphasised elsewhere in this book the hope for a positive way forward is for organisations and individuals to have a stake in the learning process.

For those historically isolated in their places of work from people and paper resources to support their learning, electronic media does open up enormous possibilities for addressing this isolation. More individuals will be able to site their learning at work and be able to maximise the opportunities electronic media presents for integrated learning. It also offers the chance for the development of wider communities of professional interest and thus services and professions generally. Whilst individuals and groups of staff can use these resources, organisations need to invest to reap the benefits.

Providers of learning opportunities need to respond to the needs of individuals and organisations and view the consumerist implication not as unwelcome but as one strand of the blurring of boundaries between education, training and leisure (Edwards, 1997, cited in Young and Marks-Moran, 1999). They will need to be responsive, creative and persuasive to win new learners in an increasingly crowded and globalised training and education market place. In such a scenario workplace learners should be the winners and, hopefully, the users of the service they work in.

References

Adams, R., Dominelli, L. and Payne, M. (Eds.) (1998) *Social Work Themes Issues and Critical Debates*, Basingstoke: Macmillan Press.

Blundell, R., Dearden, L. and Meghir, C. (1996) *The Determinants and Effects of Work Related Training in Britain*, London: The Institute for Fiscal Studies.

Bines, H. and Watson, D. (1992) *Developing Professional Education*, Buckingham: SRHE/Open University Press.

Braye, S. and Preston-Shoot, M. (1996 2nd edition) *Empowering Practice in Social Care*, Buckingham: Open University Press.

Burke, J.W. (Ed.) (1989) *Competency-based Education and Training*, London: The Falmer Press.

Carroll, Lewis (1993 edition) *Alice's Adventures in Wonderland* and *Through the Looking Glass*, Bristol: Parragon.

DfEE (1998) *The Learning Age—A Renaissance for a New Britain*, London: The Stationery Office Limited.

DfEE (1998b) *A New Approach to Learning*, http://www.dfee.gov.uk/ufi/newappr.htm 15/01/99.

DfEE (1999) *Local Information, Advice and Guidance for Adults in England—Towards a National Framework: Learning Direct—Leaflet*, http://www.lifelonglearning.co.uk/iag/iago2.htm.

DfEE (1999) *National Learning Targets for England for 2002*, http://www.dfee.gov.uk/ntt/targets.htm

DOH (1999) Social Care Group, http://www.doh.gov.uk

Eraut, M. (1994) *Developing Professional Knowledge and Competence*, London: Falmer Press.

ESWIN (1999) New NTOs, http//www.nisw.org.uk/eswinuk/uket.htm

Edwards, R. (1997) *Changing Places?* London: Routledge.

Fletcher, S. (1997) *Planning and Implementing your S/NVQ System*, London: Kogan Page Practical Trainer Series.

Frissen, P. (1997) The Virtual State—Postmodernisation, Informatisation and Public Administration, in Loader, B.D. (Ed.) *The Governance of Cyberspace Politics, Technoloy and Global Restructuring*, London: Routledge.

Fryer, R.H. (1997) *Learning for the Twenty-first Century. First Report of the National Advisory Group for Continuing Education and Lifelong Learning*, London: National Advisory Group for Continuing Education and Lifelong Learning.

Hyland, T. and Matlay, H. (1997) Small Business, Training Needs and VET Provision, *Journal of Education and Work*, Vol 10 No 2 pp. 129–139.

Jessup G. (1989) The Emerging Model of Vocational Education and Training, in Burke, J.W. (Ed.) *Competency-based Education and Training*, London: The Falmer Press.

Kingston, P. On Closer Inspection, *Guardian Education*, Tuesday, January 19, 1999, p. 13.

Lane, D. (1999) New for Kids, *The Guardian Society*, Wednesday, 13, 1999, pp. 8–9.

Larsson, S. (1997), The Meaning of Lifelong Learning, in Walters, S. (Ed.) *Globalization, Adult Education and Training Impacts and Issues*, Cape Town: Zed Books.

Lishman, J (1998) Personal and Professional Development, in Adams, R., Dominelli, L. and Payne, M. (Eds.) (1998) *Social Work Themes, Issues and Critical Debates*, Basingstoke: Macmillan Press.

Loader, B.D. (Ed.) (1997) *The Governance of Cyberspace—Politics, Technoloy and Global Restructuring*, London: Routledge.

NAGCELL (1999) *Creating Learning Cultures: Next Steps in Achieving the Learning Age*, http://www.lifelonglearning.co.uk/nagcell2/index.htm

Norton, R, (Ed.) Davies, B., Ireland, D. and Nicoll, D. (1994) *The Future of Education and Qualifications in Youth and Community Work and the Irrelevance of S/NVQs*, London: Community and Youth Workers' Union Education and Training Committee.

Payne, J. (1999) *Adults Learning*, 10 8, 9–11.

Reith, L (1998) News, *Focus*, November 1998, p. 2.

Song Seng, L and Sock Hwee, L. (1997) *An Empirical Framework for Implementing Lifelong Learning Systems*, pp. 1–14, http://www.lifelong-learning.org/law.low.htm 05/01/99.

Tait, A. and Mills, R. (Eds.) (1999) *The Convergence of Distance and Conventional Education*, London: Routledge.

University of Industry (1998) *Modernising Learning: The Role of the University of Industry*, http://www.lifelonglearning.co.uk/ufi/paper02.htm 15/01/99.

Walters, S. (Ed.) (1997) *Globalization, Adult Education and Training Impacts and Issues*, Cape Town: Zed Books.

Watson, D. (1992) The Future: Problems and Prospects, in Bines, H. and Watson, D. *Developing Professional Education*, Buckingham: SRHE/Open University Press.

Wolf, A. (1995) *Competence-based Assessment*, Buckingham: Open University Press.

Young, G. and Marks-Moran, D. (1999) A Case Study of Convergence Between Distance and Conventional Education, in Tait, A. and Mills, R. (Eds.) *The Convergence of Distance and Conventional Education*, London: Routledge.

Youth Clubs UK (1999) *Youth Achievements Awards—Questions and Answers*, http://www.youthclubs.org.uk/yaawards.html 1–13.

Youth Clubs UK *National Occupational Standards Review*, http://www.nya.org.uk/standsum.htm